YOU, YOUR HUSBAND, AND HIS MOTHER

YOU, YOUR HUSBAND

& *His*

Mother

Create a Healthy Relationship
with Your Mother-in-Law—and Your
Spouse—in Five Simple Steps

DR. TRACY DALGLEISH

TARCHER
an imprint of Penguin Random House
New York

Tarcher

an imprint of Penguin Random House LLC
1745 Broadway, New York, NY 10019
penguinrandomhouse.com

Most Tarcher books are available at a discount when purchased in
quantity for sales promotions or corporate use. Special editions, which
include personalized covers, excerpts, and corporate imprints, can be
created when purchased in large quantities. For more information, please
e-mail specialmarkets@penguinrandomhouse.com. Your local
bookstore can also assist with discounted bulk purchases using the
Penguin Random House corporate Business-to-Business program.
For assistance in locating a participating retailer,
e-mail B2B@penguinrandomhouse.com.

Book design by Shannon Nicole Plunkett

Library of Congress Cataloging-in-Publication
Data has been requested.

ISBN (hardcover): 9798217045600
ISBN (e-book): 9798217045617

Printed in the United States of America
1st Printing

The authorized representative in the EU for product safety and compliance
is Penguin Random House Ireland, Morrison Chambers, 32 Nassau Street,
Dublin D02 YH68, Ireland, https://eu-contact.penguin.ie.

This book is dedicated to everyone who dares to break old patterns and strengthen their marriage and families.

CONTENTS

INTRODUCTION

In 2011, as I was entering the last year of my PhD program in clinical psychology, I traveled to Turkey for an international conference. During a break, I roamed Istanbul's incredible Spice Bazaar. As I took in the sights of beaded bracelets, sugar-covered Turkish delight, and more bins of sumac than I could have imagined, a seller stood at the edge of his shop, calling out to patrons, "Get your spices! Candy! A beautiful scarf for your mother-in-law!" His booming voice continued without any change in intonation as I locked eyes with him: "Perhaps some poison for your mother-in-law?"

My now-husband Greg and I were then dating long distance, and I was still some time away from having a mother-in-law myself, but I did already have individual and couple clients who were struggling with that relationship. There I was, halfway around the world, and still—across culture, religion, and time—people recognized that a mother-in-law can present one of the greatest challenges for a couple.

The challenging mother-in-law has long been a popular trope. Jennifer Lopez and Jane Fonda starred opposite each other in a popular movie called *Monster-in-Law*, in which Fonda fears losing her son to Lopez and intentionally creates problems in hopes of breaking them up. Taylor Swift had an international hit with "Anti-Hero," in which she sings about a nightmare that her someday-daughter-in-law will kill her for her money. On social media, viral videos call out everything from "mammismo," the intense bond between Italian mothers and sons, to "mother-in-law math," the "unspoken rules" that mothers-in-law create to blame family problems on their daughters-in-law.[1]

Almost every day of my clinical practice, individuals and couples come to me in enormous distress over a tridirectional dynamic they have no idea how to navigate—one that is undermining their family *and* their marriage. Readers of my first book, *I Didn't Sign Up for This*, message me in despair about the family they married into, while on my social media and Be Connected Digital platforms, people daily ask for help with a mother-in-law who doesn't respect boundaries, makes divisive comments, or uses guilt trips and manipulation to get her needs met. My clients have no idea how to bridge the gap in generational parenting styles or how to deflect their mother-in-law's criticisms. They don't want to be the person responsible for communicating and connecting with their husband's family of origin, especially when the role comes with vitriol or disrespect from a mother-in-law who doesn't treat them as part of that family. Many feel completely overwhelmed making logistical decisions to accommodate their empty-nester mother-in-law while receiving no accommodations themselves as they parent small children.

These women are often boundary bosses in other areas of their life. They've navigated professional careers; they've developed a fairer division of labor in their marriages; they're assertive and confident with their friends. But when it comes to their mother-in-law, they struggle.

The greatest challenge to creating change is the common misperception that the only options are victim and villain. That if the wife advocates for herself or her children, she's becoming a villain toward her mother-in-law *and* her husband. Or that to appease others and keep the peace, the wife must be a constant victim, placating toxic cycles of guilt and gaslighting. Since neither of these positions feels good for the wife (or her husband

and family), I guide my clients to use a different approach: my VAULT method. Instead of allowing you to end up stuck as the villain or victim, my system invites you, the daughter-in-law, to become your *own* main character and take a seat at the table, in a place that aligns with and prioritizes your marriage.

A caveat: This is *not* a book about vilifying the evil mother-in-law. There are many deeply meaningful relationships built between mothers-in-law and daughters-in-law, and the strategies you will learn in this book can strengthen a couple's approach to navigating extended family. At the same time, I acknowledge that this dynamic is complex and requires an approach that examines the individual, the couple, and their family dynamics.

When I polled my online community, 85 percent of women said they have conflict with their partner about their mother-in-law. Couples come into my office heading toward divorce because they do not have a solution for navigating their mother-in-law problems.

I get where my clients and online community are coming from. I've been there with my own husband and mother-in-law. It has been a journey, but I can now say we are stronger as a couple and as a family (including both families of origin). We've had to sit in conversations that were filled with tension, looking at ourselves and our patterns, all with a deep desire to experience something different that felt better for us as a couple. This is hard work that we wouldn't have been able to achieve without our commitment to ourselves and our marriage.

Yes, this dynamic is challenging. But if you face it as a team, you can strengthen your partnership *and* improve your interactions with your MIL. This work can be a path forward to greater connection with your husband and help you get your needs met as a member of this family. Instead of increasing conflict, you'll learn how to increase connection while holding your boundaries and respecting your needs.

I promise, both things are possible.

DOING SOMETHING DIFFERENT

Over the next ten chapters, I'll take you through my system to help address even the trickiest situations with your mother-in-law. Dysfunctional family patterns commonly occur without our awareness. They are repetitive and consistent. As is the case with many of my clients, your husband may not be aware of these cycles yet, which can make starting this work difficult—but not impossible. Every day I work with individuals and couples who are creating real change.

This book is divided into two parts. In part I, I identify the challenges unique to this triangle. Based on my years of clinical practice, I help you identify which style of daughter-in-law you are, which type of mother-in-law you're dealing with, and how to take productive—not divisive—action. I outline common dysfunctional family patterns, including strategies your husband may be using that prevent him from seeing his mother's behavior for what it is. I also provide step-by-step instructions to help you and your husband get out of your negative communication cycles. By the end of part I, couples will have a blueprint for achieving greater intimacy and connection as they practice building a healthy new way of connecting: interdependence.

In part II, I teach you my five-step VAULT method chapter by chapter, empowering you with evidence-based psychotherapy interventions, behavioral and communication strategies, and organizational change principles. Why "VAULT"? A vault is strong, secure, and protective—just as a couple's relationship must be. It represents an unshakable foundation of trust and mutual understanding. When a vault is intact, it keeps what matters most—love, connection, and shared values—protected from outside forces. Using the five steps, you and your spouse will identify your shared values, define the in-law relationships you aspire to, achieve a deeper understanding of your triangle dynamics, identify your limits and boundaries, and finally take action with all your new skills firmly in place. In the last chapter,

I provide answers and scripts to the most common questions I get. By the end, you'll be able to move past the victim/villain binary with a plan for creating lasting change with your MIL as part of your newly strengthened marriage.

A NOTE ABOUT HOW THIS BOOK IS WRITTEN

You're going to meet several people throughout the following pages. These are composite characters created from the core experiences of my real-life clients' stories. To ensure confidentiality, all identifying information has been changed, but their dynamics with their mothers-in-law, coping mechanisms, and relationship outcomes are preserved to show you how real people used these tools and strategies to make meaningful change.

Although this book is written for daughters-in-law dealing with mothers-in-law, the VAULT method is one that any couple can use with any extended family members. Perhaps you're dealing with a problematic father-in-law or sister-in-law, or perhaps it's your own mother you and your partner are struggling with. This book can still provide help.

I also want to note that I've written from my perspective as a heterosexual cisgender person, which also represents the majority of my clients. I don't want to imply that the issues I focus on in the book are the same for every couple; sometimes dynamics that are common in straight relationships are not common in LGBTQ ones, and vice versa. While the specific gender-related issues presented in this book may not apply to everyone, the VAULT system can still offer valuable tools and resources for all.

And lastly, I will use the common acronyms MIL (mother-in-law) and DIL (daughter-in-law) throughout the book.

Let's get started.

PART I

The Challenges

Chapter 1

A SPECIAL KIND
OF RELATIONSHIP

*B*ecky and Cliff are at a standstill in my office—again. They're a couple in their late thirties with two young kids, and Becky is insisting Cliff speak to his mother regarding her habit of constantly buying their kids gifts, especially items that Becky and Cliff have already vetoed. "We agreed no smartphone until high school," Becky says. "And she knew that."

Cliff sighs and looks at the ceiling. As he does this, I notice Becky's eyes widen in frustration as she fumbles to find the words to speak up for herself. Cliff's argument? His mother's gifts are "well-intentioned." Although Becky feels like this is something that only she and her husband are struggling with, it echoes a daily debate in my therapy room about control—who has it and who's trying to seize it.

While Cliff is a willing partner in couples therapy, another client of mine, Helena, attends therapy alone because her husband, Shawn, doesn't see the value. Shawn continues to tell her that she just needs to accept who his mother is because she'll "never change"—meaning he won't ask her to change. Even after an incident where his mother insisted that their six-week-old should be sleeping in his own room because she was against co-sleeping. That particular conversation took a turn when Shawn's mother said to Helena, "You're going to make this whole family sick by continuing to share a bed."

Shawn remained silent, unwilling to see his mother's impact on his wife. Helena, however, boiled over. While their three-year-old cried to be picked up by her overwhelmed mother, Helena shouted at her mother-in-law to stop disrespecting her and leave their family home. Subsequently, Helena was overcome by feelings of shame for having shown this side of herself in front of her children, fury that her husband remained silent, and resentment that at some point her husband would invite his mother back into their home.

In my clinical practice, online programs, and interactions with friends and colleagues, one issue comes up more frequently than any other: unresolved mother-in-law conflict. With all the progress we've made toward healthier, more equitable marriages, you might think we should have moved past this age-old conflict between mother-in-law and daughter-in-law. I can definitively say that we have not.

In my clinical practice, I encounter women every single day who struggle to find solutions to dealing with their mother-in-law. I also receive an outpouring of comments and private messages from women in my online community, Be Connected Digital, anytime I talk about the mother-in-law dilemma. What is striking is that many of these women are assertive and confident in other roles. Many hold professional degrees. Many navigate the multiple demands required to raise young children. Many have built six-figure businesses. Yet some of the fiercest and most confident women struggle in their relationships with their mothers-in-law.

While the details of my clients' stories vary, at the root of their issues is the same question: How do I keep our marriage strong and change this relationship with my mother-in-law?

THE MOTHER-SON RELATIONSHIP

Carly, a new mother attempting to cope with postpartum anxiety, came to me because she was having nightmares that her mother-in-law wanted to steal her baby. When I probed further, I discovered that her fears weren't wholly irrational. Her mother-in-law regularly made comments like "You're just a distraction to my son. You aren't my grandson's real family. My grandson's real family is his father, his aunt, and me."

I try to keep my emotions well hidden in session, but I could feel the anger rise in my throat. Carly's nervous system was urging her to protect her child, and her unconscious mind was trying to work out how another woman could speak to her this way. Furthermore, her marriage was beginning to crumble, as whenever she approached her husband about her fears, he didn't believe her and brushed her off.

Carly's story is similar to those of many of my clients, and it told me clearly that this mother-in-law could not even begin to fathom the idea of healthy individuation between herself and her son or view her son as a separate autonomous being with his own family. Carly's mother-in-law seemed to view her daughter-in-law as a threat to maintaining the family bond she wanted. But Carly felt stuck because she couldn't simply end the relationship. After all, this was her husband's mother.

Part of what makes the mother-in-law relationship so challenging to navigate is its unique characteristics within a family unit. The MIL is not part of the nuclear, or chosen, family and most often (in Western society) doesn't live with the family or participate in their daily decision-making. Yet the MIL can wreak havoc on the couple's relational bond and turn even the sturdiest marriages upside down. Unlike friends, colleagues, or that distant uncle, the MIL isn't someone a couple can easily shut out of their life, nor might they want to. But a wrong move can result in hurt feelings and heated arguments. A rejected suggestion can trigger an onslaught of passive-aggressive comments and guilt trips. A boundary being set can unintentionally lead to an estrangement.

These experiences can all be heightened depending on whether your partner is able to step into your experience and understand what is happening from your perspective or is shutting down and unaware of the established patterns. When mother and adult child are highly fused, it can feel impossible to find a solution. For your husband, this is the woman who birthed him, who nurtured him from dependency into adulthood, who was there when he took his first steps and hugged him when he wasn't picked for the soccer team. As a mother, I recognize that I am my son's first relationship with a woman. A mother helps teach her child what it means to love, to share emotions and needs, to feel physically connected and safe with another person. This is a key relationship in a boy's life.

But children grow up.

Working with couples clinically for nearly two decades, I notice that women often learn to individuate and set boundaries with their family of origin at an earlier age. It's more acceptable for the "moody" teenage daughter to yell at her mother, tell her off, and say no. She rages against her mother, asserts her differences, or writes in her diary about how she'll get away someday. Boys, however, tend to struggle with separation and boundary setting with their family.

One way I understand this is through attachment styles. People generally exhibit one of four attachment styles: anxious-preoccupied (characterized by fear of rejection and a need for constant reassurance), dismissive-avoidant (characterized by overvaluing independence and self-reliance), fearful-avoidant (characterized by a desire for deep closeness with a simultaneous fear of emotional intimacy), and secure (characterized by healthy interdependence and open communication). Research shows that rates of avoidant attachment style tend to be higher for men. On the positive side, this can make them resilient and good problem solvers. But they are also more likely to stuff down their feelings and not share their needs with significant others.

Another way I understand this is through societal messaging. Men are often taught from early infancy to pull up their socks and not vocalize painful emotions. I remember noticing that my son's well-intentioned grandparents often told him to "brush it off" when he hurt himself. I was surprised two years later when my daughter joined the family and received messages of empathy and soothing in the same situations. This early messaging leads men not to express their emotions or share their needs. As a result, I tend to see men in later adulthood not only struggling to identify their moment-to-moment needs but also failing to say no and assert their wishes with their mother.

What does this look like for a man once a life partner enters the picture? He might simply ignore troublesome texts from his mother instead of responding to them and advocating for himself or his partner. Instead of asking questions when his mother guilt-trips him, he might leave the room or start looking at his phone. Instead of setting limits with his mother about what she does when caring for her grandkids, he'll make excuses for her behavior so he won't have to say anything to her. While this avoidance may have worked well enough when he was single, he now has a front-row witness who is being profoundly affected by his inaction.

Somewhat paradoxically, just because someone exhibits avoidant behaviors doesn't mean they've achieved a healthy independence from their family of origin. Although they may be self-sufficient adults, people who avoid thinking or talking about these issues can't fully individuate from their families, and they continue to be fused to their parents. Emotional fusion may sound like it just means being really close to someone, but it's actually the *opposite* of what we're aiming for in healthy relationships.

A term from psychiatrist Dr. Murray Bowen's family systems theory, *fusion* is the experience of abandoning our desires, wants, and needs in the hopes of pleasing, fixing, and placating others.[1]

An individual who's fused with their parents experiences psychological enmeshment and codependency; their thoughts, feelings, and behaviors are entangled with those of their parents such that it is hard to see the individual "I." While emotional fusion and codependency can offer a short-term sense of relief, in the long run, they end up creating more conflict and mental distress within the individual and the family system.

Instead of living in emotional fusion, we must work toward being healthily individuated, which means we can recognize that we have our own thoughts and feelings that are different from those of our family members and that we may choose to act in ways that they may not. Individuation means simultaneously holding two truths in mind: (1) I am okay as I am, and (2) you may not like who I am, and that is also okay. This approach meets a core need that we have in any relationship: to feel that our thoughts and emotions are considered and that we have power (over our own actions, not the other person's). Individuation is a key piece to building interdependence in all relationships.

What is interdependence? Interdependence is the balance between autonomy and interconnectedness, which acknowledges that each person in a relationship has a separate identity, both of which must be valued and respected, while supporting each other's needs. An interdependent relationship doesn't involve power struggles or manipulation or trying to prove whose wishes are more important than whose. In a family system, it's about co-creating a world together from a place that acknowledges that each person has their own thoughts, feelings, desires, opinions, and values, all while finding ways to prioritize connection, collaboration, and compromise.

VICTIM OR VILLAIN

To compound the challenges described above, four different dynamics are operating in any conflict with a mother-in-law: the relationship between mother and son, the relationship between mother-in-law and daughter-in-law, the relationship between husband and wife, and the couple's relationship with the mother-in-law. As they try to navigate the complexities involved, women often fall prey to remaining in a binary role: They're either the victim or the villain.

When a woman doesn't stand up for herself, she feels like a victim, asking, "Why does my mother-in-law do this to me? And why can't my husband see it?" Feeling powerless and stuck, she begins to buy into the narrative that her desires and boundaries do not matter. She maintains a "good girl" disposition and does not speak up for herself. Any sense of tension leads her to retract her wishes and placate her MIL, telling herself, "I should be grateful, she's family. Many people wish they had family around." However, this self-sacrifice creates *more* distress in the marriage, not less. A woman in the victim role stays stuck because she doesn't have a way to find her own sense of agency in the triangle with her husband and his mother.

Eventually, in reaction to this loss of agency, some women try to make a change and stand up for themselves. But whether they calmly try to set boundaries or lash out in anger, they often end up feeling like—or being labeled as—the villain. A woman in the villain role will say things like "My MIL thinks I'm causing all these problems in her family," "My MIL blames me for my husband not calling her," or "I'm the scapegoat because I refuse to take my child to a family dinner with people swearing at each other." The behavior of both her MIL and her husband leads her to feel that she has no other choice than to be the "bad guy." She ends up feeling like anything she says or does is wrong—but if she goes back to the role of victim, she doesn't feel any better, and the conflicts with her MIL still aren't resolved.

Within both the victim and villain roles, women often believe they're doing what's necessary to avoid damage to their marriage. Yet staying stuck in these roles, unable to resolve MIL-related conflicts, frequently leads to divorce.

I believe it doesn't have to reach that point. You *can* find a clear path through this struggle, one that allows you to have a seat at the table and to form a solid team with your partner. My five-step VAULT method will help you pull yourself out of the victim/villain binary so you and your partner can create a stronger bond with each other and a united front in dealing with your MIL, while also appreciating the bond between mother and son.

THE SIX TYPES OF MOTHER-IN-LAW

After a decade of research as a clinical psychologist and nearly two decades of working with thousands of clients, I have come to notice repeated patterns that show up between my clients and their mothers-in-law in personality characteristics, communication habits, and behaviors. Based on these patterns, I have identified six types of mothers-in-law (which fall into three categories) and three styles of daughters-in-law.

Without understanding the type of MIL you have, you might be engaging in patterns of communication with your husband or MIL that are inadvertently creating more distress, defensiveness, and divisiveness. But the dynamic that unfolds between people is not static and can change. Awareness and understanding are always the first steps. Identifying your MIL's traits and behaviors as well as your own will help you start to move through conflict and strengthen your relationship.

Broadly, the three categories of MILs are: Internalizers (those who focus on themselves), Externalizers (those who focus on criticizing their daughters-in-law), and Balancers (those who can see both their own and their DIL's viewpoints). As you'll see, each of these categories is further divided into two different types. Even if your MIL doesn't fit neatly into a single type, reading through these categories helps you identify certain patterns your MIL embodies and how she interacts with her son and with you. These types are not a diagnosis but rather a way to understand themes of behavior to help you navigate the complexities of this relationship.

Note that "narcissist" is not one of the types, though many of the behaviors described overlap with those of a narcissist—someone who guilt-trips you, lacks empathy, feels a baseless sense of envy or competition, puts you down, criticizes you, and plays the victim. While this label can be incredibly helpful for some, I often move away from it, as (a) people can exhibit some narcissistic behaviors without meeting the criteria for clinical narcissism, and (b) your husband could be deeply hurt by anyone labeling his mother as a narcissist, which will only make the overall problem harder to solve.

Now let's dive into breaking down the different types of MILs, so we can start to identify ways of communicating and boundaries that will be more helpful.

THE INTERNALIZERS

The first category of mother-in-law we'll look at is the Internalizers. These are MILs who are less focused on tearing down their daughters-in-law and more focused on themselves—but not in a healthy way. I divide this category into two types: the Martyr and the Victim.

The Martyr

The Martyr type of mother-in-law presents as dutiful and giving, with a bottomless bucket of care for her family. But her help isn't given freely; it's laden with guilt or obligation. In fact, although she seems to want approval, the Martyr often goes out of her way to put herself in situations where she'll end up feeling unappreciated, because it confirms her view of herself as self-sacrificing. For example, she might offer to help with something but do it in a way that isn't actually helpful or on a timeline that doesn't work for you.

Becky's MIL is a classic Martyr. She frequently agrees to watch her grandchildren but then complains to Becky and Cliff about how exhausted she is afterward. She chooses gifts that the couple has vetoed (such as smartphones), then feels upset that the kids aren't using them. When Becky and Cliff aren't available for Sunday night dinner, she sees them as ungrateful and cancels her visit to see the kids during the week. Yet it's confusing to her when Becky turns down her offers of support, because how could someone not want her support?

The Martyr exudes passive-aggressive behavior but can't admit to it, which also contributes to her repressed resentment toward others. She might say things like "I try so hard, but I guess I can never get it right with you" or "After all I've done for you, I can't believe you'd treat me this way." Any attempt to rationalize with her will likely be met with denial and minimization of your experience. She will say things like "How could you think that?" or "I just want what's best for the family"—seeing herself as a selfless do-gooder, when in fact she's likely causing more problems than she's solving. You might find yourself responding to the Martyr by giving in to her demands out of guilt, overexplaining your wants and needs to her, or trying to convince her how much you appreciate her.

The Victim

The Victim MIL experiences life as if everything is happening *to* her and believes she has no control over her choices. Unlike the Martyr, who believes her ongoing self-sacrifice goes unappreciated, the Victim simply feels like the outside world is a personal attack on her and that others are out to exploit her.

Julie and Damion are trying to navigate a Victim MIL. Damion's mother feels everyone and everything is out to "pull her down," from the contractor who didn't finish the basement renovation to medical complications from an unmanaged chronic health condition to Damion's father, who left the family decades ago. Of course, all these are unfortunate situations, but in her mind, they all happened *to* her without any recognition of her own participation or the actions she could take to make things better. She complains to Julie and Damion, which pulls on Damion's inner desire to be a "good son" and care for his mother.

Because the Victim exerts so little agency in her life, other family members get sucked into the "rescuer" role, like Damion trying to alleviate his mother's distress at all hours. Even those who don't directly enable the drama often indirectly enable it by making excuses like "That's just Mom. You know how she is." All the while, other family members' needs end up getting pushed to the side—especially the daughter-in-law's. You might notice yourself responding to the Victim by trying to fix everything for her, giving her advice that inadvertently assumes she can't make her own choices, or oversympathizing with her, which keeps her stuck in the role of the Victim.

THE EXTERNALIZERS

While Internalizers like the Martyr and the Victim consciously or unconsciously make everything about themselves, Externalizers focus on the actions of others—especially their daughters-in-law. This externalization usually takes the form of finding fault with others or telling them what to do, which is why I divide Externalizers into two types: the Blamer and the Controller.

The Blamer

True to her name, the Blamer MIL blames any difficulties she experiences on other people, and when it comes to family problems, that usually means her daughter-in-law. Instead of looking at dysfunction in her own behavior or in the overall family dynamic, the Blamer uses her DIL as the scapegoat, saying things like "We didn't have these problems before you." In most cases, the problems were there before you joined the family, but they were easier to ignore when the relationship between mother and son was characterized by obedience, placation, or straight-up avoidance. When the Blamer's son got married and that relationship dynamic shifted, she viewed it as the start of the problem. She might even view her son as "the golden child"—and her DIL as the "black sheep" who turned her son against her.

Helena's MIL, for example, blames Helena for the missed dinners and family gatherings. She doesn't believe her son would set boundaries like "Mom, we're not bringing our four-week-old on a six-hour car drive to see you" if it weren't for Helena's influence.

A common toxic dynamic that shows up with the Blamer is triangulation. Instead of communicating directly with her DIL about an issue, she complains to her son, putting him in the middle of the conflict and trying to get him to side with her, like Helena's MIL complaining to her son about how she didn't think Helena was a competent mother. Or, conversely, instead of communicating with her son, the MIL complains to her DIL about something her son is doing or not doing. For example, Helena's MIL asks her if her son is taking his vitamins and watching his diet, as if Helena were responsible for the health of her husband, a grown adult. In your dynamic with your Blamer MIL, without realizing it, you might respond to her with defensiveness, over-apologize to her in order to sidestep conflict, or try to convince her of the validity of your wishes or actions (often to no avail).

The Controller

The Controller is always right. Unlike the Martyr, she doesn't self-sacrifice or give up her own time to care for her grandchildren, but she is the first to criticize your parenting. Her backhanded remarks put you down without acknowledging that you have your own needs or desires that are different from hers. When trying to set boundaries, you end up in debates about parenting and overall life decisions in which she dismisses your viewpoint and tries to one-up you with her so-called expertise. She acts as if she knows better than you about everything, including your husband. She might say things like "This is how we do it in our family/culture" in an attempt to assert matriarchal dominance and strong-arm you into doing things her way.

Melanie's MIL is a classic Controller. She arrives for non-negotiable monthlong visits and insists on staying at their house, which is already crowded enough with three children. She only speaks Italian to her son and dictates all family plans over the holidays. When confronted with alternative ideas, she brushes them aside by saying that this is how things are done in her family. She tells everyone what to do, including Melanie's kids, and judges Melanie's parenting style at every turn, insisting her own parenting methods "worked just fine." With the Controller MIL, it's common for daughters-in-law to overexplain or overjustify themselves (which results in porous boundaries), to ask for permission unnecessarily, or to simply avoid conflict all together.

THE BALANCERS

Unlike Internalizers (who are all about themselves) and Externalizers (who are all about criticizing and controlling others), Balancers understand that both parties in a relationship have their own perspectives and needs. This is, of course, a much healthier attitude overall, but even so, problems can still present themselves, so it's helpful to think about the dynamics in play.

The Distancer

Unlike with the types of mothers-in-law described above, you probably won't be having much conflict with a Distancer—but you probably won't have many positive interactions with her either. In fact, she is so absent from the relationship that you probably won't interact with her much at all. When a family history of avoidance prevails in the mother-child relationship, the result can be a Distancer who remains more or less out of the picture once the adult child is with a partner.

For some daughters-in-law, this works fine, as they don't long to have an involved parental figure. But others may wish they could rely on "one more parent" to support them, especially when they have kids of their own. For example, Jenny and Clay were focused on traveling in the early years of their relationship and didn't see much need for his mother to be involved in their life. However, now that they have a child and busy entrepreneurial careers, they wish they had the proverbial village to rely on.

The Distancer may be open to establishing a closer relationship, but she may also understand that this is who she is and ask her child and his partner to accept that this is the role she would prefer to play in their life. When your MIL is a Distancer, you might end up personalizing her actions (or inactions), overextending yourself in an attempt to include her in your family, or avoiding contact because you assume she's not interested at all.

The Supporter

One client, Jamila, described "hitting the lottery" with her mother-in-law. When she gave birth to her second child, her MIL was eager to jump in, caring for the home while Jamila juggled two kids under two. Her MIL would respectfully ask what she needed and ensure that Jamila knew what she was doing (unlike the Martyr, who does tasks to feel noble rather than to actually be helpful). When heated moments came up between Jamila and her husband, her MIL would provide a listening ear without interfering or taking sides.

Yes, this dream is possible! But all relationships require attention and communication to stay healthy. The challenge with the Supporter is that, on one hand, she might be so conscious of respecting boundaries that, in an effort not to intrude, she might become too removed. On the other hand, if she's less conscious of boundaries and you set one, her feelings might be temporarily hurt. On your end, as you interact with the Supporter MIL, you might avoid asserting your desires or needs out of gratitude for her support, or you might assume your MIL is okay when she's not, simply as a result of this dynamic with her. Jamila and her MIL are both learning how to co-create their relationship through clear communication. This also requires Jamila and her husband to talk about their needs and wishes ahead of spending time with his family. With this bit of effort, everyone involved is able to find a healthy balance.

WHAT STYLE OF DAUGHTER-IN-LAW ARE YOU?

Now that you've thought about what type of mother-in-law you have, it's important to consider the traits and characteristics that you bring to the relationship as a daughter-in-law. We all bring perceptions, assumptions, and coping mechanisms into all our relationships, including those with our MILs. Identifying your strengths and challenges as a DIL empowers you to understand the behaviors or thought patterns that contribute to the dynamic with your MIL, including those that might be keeping you stuck. When we understand our own processes and tendencies, we are more able to respond to difficult situations in an intentional way rather than reacting from a triggered and emotional place.

Through working with people, I have noticed three distinct styles of DILs: Good Girls, Managers, and Collaborators. I want to emphasize the intentional use of the word *style* here. While you might identify predominantly with one style, these are not immutable personality traits, and you can learn to shift into a different style. (Your MIL can change her behavior too, but you can't change it for her, which is why I've used the word *types* for MILs.) The important thing is that by gaining an awareness of how you show up in your relationship with your MIL, you'll be able to problem solve key parts of your own behavior that might be getting in the way of a functional relationship.

I don't say this to place blame on how you show up in the world. Whichever style of DIL you are, you doubtless have many strengths. It's just that when it comes to creating healthy interdependent relationships, we want to ensure that we have access to many different approaches. Otherwise, it's like having a toolbox that only contains a hammer; that works great sometimes, but we want to have other tools available to us when the situation calls for them. Learning about the different DIL styles will help you recognize a dynamic as it's unfolding and give you a deeper sense of agency to change that dynamic when appropriate.

THE GOOD GIRL

Every summer, Lauren and her husband would pack up the kids and make the fourteen-hour drive to the cottage where they would stay with Lauren's mother-in-law for four weeks. It was a lovely lake house, and Lauren knew it was what her MIL wanted. "It's tradition," she told me. "It's just what we do in the family." But as her story unfolded, it became apparent that this annual vacation was anything but relaxing. Between visits from neighbors she didn't know well, vigilantly keeping her kids safe around water, and making sure her kids didn't make a mess of the cottage's expensive white decor, Lauren was tired, but she kept going in order to make her husband's family happy. While her caring nature was admirable, she was sacrificing every single summer vacation, trying to convince herself that the exhaustion was just to be expected. Lauren was a classic Good Girl.

The Good Girl is favored, as she easily says yes, responds to text messages, and makes plans with both sides of the family. She seems to effortlessly give and bend to the requests of others, particularly her MIL. Her caring disposition is a strength, one that is highly valued in society. Many women long to be seen and supported, especially by those of older generations, and Good Girls believe, consciously or not, that they can achieve this by performing the roles they're expected to perform without complaint.

Good Girls' tendency to say yes to any request stems from a desire to please, a need to receive external validation from others, and a deep-rooted fear of being unlovable. The internalized belief often sounds like "If others are happy and I am liked, then I am worthy and good enough." Yet in working hard to please others, they often neglect to set any boundaries, readily agreeing to do things they actually can't or don't want to do.

The cost of the Good Girl's self-denial is a slow, simmering resentment and a real potential for burnout. When we abandon our own desires in the service of others, anger, envy, or exhaustion can start to build. Some might feel a sense of being owed something in return for their agreeable disposition, and they get upset when the reward never comes. Others fall into feeling like a victim; they feel these experiences keep happening to them and they have no choice but to please others and say yes.

Good Girls often care deeply about the emotions of others, including their MILs. Lauren, for example, sensed the sadness and disappointment her MIL felt when they weren't able to visit her, so she tried to overcompensate with longer visits to the lake house, even though those visits made her miserable. While the Good Girl's empathy is admirable, she too often ignores her own feelings. Her porous boundaries lead her not to make space for her needs. I like to remind Good Girls that if someone isn't communicating their needs, they're abandoning themselves.

When dealing with her MIL and creating healthy boundaries alongside her partner, the Good Girl needs to stop seeking external validation and turn inward to give herself validation. Practice asking yourself if saying yes to something will make you happy in the long run or if it's just less trouble in the short term. Exploring the true costs of abandoning yourself is key. I recommend practicing setting down others' needs: Instead of juggling the balls that represent your MIL's disappointment or upset feelings, let them drop to the ground, because they're not your sole responsibility to carry.

THE MANAGER

Marta and her husband struggled with his mother's dominating presence in their life. She always had something to say about their lifestyle choices, especially when they became parents. As the Manager style of daughter-in-law, Marta dealt with her MIL the same way she did most things in life: She vocalized every want and desire, held high standards, and clearly communicated how tasks should be completed. Marta was right to be angry at her MIL's criticisms; however, her need for control made it so that trying to have a conversation with her MIL was like bringing hot and cold air together: A storm always followed.

Managers' perfectionistic tendencies can be positive; they're achievers and natural doers. True to their name, Managers can easily step into leadership and decision-making roles. But sometimes they might lean too far in and end up micromanaging. They have high expectations not just for themselves but also for others, and when people don't meet their standards, it upsets them. They crave the certainty of being in control, but no one can be fully in control of other people or situations.

The Manager's desire for certainty is a protective mechanism, a way to cope with challenging circumstances and the unknowns that life brings. It offers her relief from a general fear of failure or of things going awfully wrong—a pattern she likely learned in early childhood. But it can also make it hard for her to compromise. Unlike Good Girls, whose boundaries are overly flexible, Managers' boundaries may be overly rigid. Marta, for example, had conflicts with her MIL over the regimented nap schedules she preferred for her kids, which her MIL didn't see the benefits of.

In the extended family dynamic, the Manager often feels like the villain or is labeled the "bad guy" by her MIL. It's not that she's "bad" but rather that her difficulties tapping into a healthy sense of flexibility end up clashing with others' sense of autonomy, triggering more tension. She can find it difficult to let others take the lead or to have patience while her husband finds his own assertiveness and starts to establish new patterns with his mother.

Managers may benefit from noticing when high rigidity heightens conflict instead of resolving it. It's possible to loosen the reins in a way that doesn't abandon your values and to work toward an inner sense of cohesion between your needs and others'. Sometimes it can be helpful to focus on the bigger picture instead of the minutiae.

THE COLLABORATOR

A classic Collaborator, Heather described herself as a family unifier and practiced balancing the needs of her kids, her husband, her mother-in-law, and herself. Heather had had many battles with her MIL, especially after her father-in-law died and her MIL transitioned to living with Heather and her husband in their family home. Yet despite the ruptures, Heather always worked toward repair, prioritizing her value of having her children be close with their grandmother.

A Collaborator is firm in her boundaries yet flexible when she needs to be, can hold a strong space for her MIL to play a role in her family life, and has built an interdependent relationship with both her husband and her MIL. She wants to share the experience of family and community. She is willing to identify what is most important to her while also seeing that she doesn't need to have control over every aspect of the family.

You might read this section and think, "I tried to be a Collaborator, but my MIL made it too difficult." I want to validate this. It's entirely likely that you started out as a Collaborator, wanting to have an involved MIL, but over time, you might have been pulled into either the Good Girl or the Manager style. This doesn't make you "bad"; it means you built adaptive strategies in response to the situation you were in—and you can always build new ones, which you'll learn how to do in this book.

While the Collaborator has largely figured out how to navigate her MIL (and maybe even has a Balancer MIL), it is important for her to slow down and consider her own values. You might pause to reflect on what truly matters to you and spend more time fully exploring your needs. Do you easily give up the individual "I" in the service of the family unit? Depending on the context, this may or may not be serving you.

FINDING A NEW SYSTEM

No matter what type of mother-in-law you have, and no matter what style of daughter-in-law you are, you can make a change in the relationship between you, your husband, and his mother. You *can* have a positive relationship with your partner while navigating the dynamics with your MIL. You *can* have a seat at the table instead of feeling you have to play the victim or the villain. You *can* build a healthy, adaptive approach in which you and your partner become good communicators, feel like an aligned and connected team, and structure your relationship with his family so that it works for both of you.

Becky and Cliff, whom we met at the beginning of the chapter, worked alongside me in therapy, implementing the VAULT method I'll outline in part II. Cliff opened up to seeing his mother's comments in a new light, and even though Becky had to learn she couldn't control her mother-in-law, Cliff's newfound awareness increased his ability to empathize with and validate Becky's reactions. They uncovered what was most important to them as a couple and agreed on various actions to address his mother's behavior. Cliff felt more empowered to set boundaries with his mother and to respond assertively to her claims of martyrdom. The couple felt like a team and was no longer stuck in their downward spiral of fighting over who was right and who was wrong. And this result also impacted their parenting positively: They found more moments of joy with their children, and their time spent with extended family was more harmonious.

This book will show you how to do the same.

Chapter 2

THE FAMILY YOU JOIN

A llison was frenzied when she arrived in my office just days before Mother's Day. In her mid-thirties with two children under five years old, she presented a specific challenge: She was on the hunt for the "perfect" gift for her mother-in-law. But as she spoke, it became clear that she wasn't looking for a gift out of kindness and generosity. Rather, she was driven by an ulterior motive: to please and perform.

It turned out that William, her husband, had never bought his mother a gift on Mother's Day. But this wasn't the only thing that stood out about William's relationship with his mother. He was the only one of her three kids who lived in a different city, and she often made passive-aggressive remarks about him "leaving" her and the rest of the family (or about Allison "taking him away"). She also had a tendency to call him and complain about things his father or siblings did, as if trying to get him to participate in family life by drawing him into drama or guilting him into showing sympathy for her. Rather than try to address these problems directly, William simply kept his mother at arm's length emotionally. And so, of her own volition, Allison took on the role of tending to his mother's feelings because she saw her husband only creating more distance from his mother.

In fact, Allison had taken on the role of the Good Girl daughter-in-law in more ways than one. In the family group chat, she updated everyone on the kids' recent activities and milestones. She sent personal thank-you notes to her MIL for the kids' gifts. She would go above and beyond to ensure William's mother's needs were met at every visit. But there was no reciprocation. Instead, her MIL found a way to criticize and blame Allison at every turn. When Allison made her MIL's favorite tourtière recipe for dinner, her MIL pushed it away, saying she "couldn't possibly eat one more fatty meal." When Allison went to her usual Saturday afternoon yoga class during her in-laws' visit, her MIL muttered, "It must be nice to get to rest."

"So what can I get her?" Allison asked me. "What will she like?"

"What are you trying to accomplish with this gift?" I asked her.

She sat and thought for a minute. "I'm trying to be the perfect daughter-in-law to make up for the problems between her and William. But it never works. I'm tired of trying to please her, and I'm tired of feeling not good enough."

This was the moment Allison began to see what so many of my clients eventually realize: She had entered a family dynamic that existed long before she married her husband.

In this chapter, we're going to look at the key factors in your relationship with your MIL that were set in motion before you even met. You'll learn about ten common toxic family dynamics that might be at the root of your problems with your MIL and husband. There's a good chance you've noticed some of these dynamics already, because you're new to the family system and not as desensitized to these patterns as your husband is, though you might not have the words to describe them. But before we start labeling these dynamics, let's look at their root causes, which include trauma, repeated cycles, and cultural norms and values. All these factors play a role in what your husband experienced growing up and in what patterns he and your MIL continue to reenact today.

BEFORE YOU JOINED THE FAMILY

Allison's dilemma is a common one for the women I work with: They try to connect with their MIL with the best intentions, only to be barraged with negativity, conflict, and exclusion. Whether it's communicated verbally or nonverbally, this rejection can lead you to ask, "Is it me?"

Probably not.

While we will explore how your actions matter in the three-sided relationship between you, your husband, and his mother in chapter 3, it's necessary to understand what existed before you joined the family and how what you're experiencing likely would have happened to any partner your spouse chose.

Each family member exists within the context of the greater family system. This context includes genetics and other biological determinants; personality traits; early childhood experiences; relationship experiences with parents, siblings, friends, and extended family members; societal and cultural messaging; and socioeconomic factors. All of these contribute to an individual's implicit (and often unconscious) understanding of three things: who I am in and of myself, who I am in relation to another person, and whether the world is a safe place.

Family dynamics are the long-standing patterns among relatives—their ways of interacting with one another and the roles that each person plays. Several factors contribute to the shaping of these interactions, including trauma, patterns of communication, personality traits, and emotional and social intelligence.

Researchers have identified several key aspects that positively influence a family to build healthy roles and dynamics, including autonomy, individuation, flexibility, respect, healthy communication, and mutuality. In fact, mutuality—the experience of cohesion between two people who are both contributing meaningfully to a relationship—has been identified as one of the strongest factors that contributes to healthy dynamics.[1] Families that are able to successfully integrate another person (like a daughter-in-law) into their system prioritize reciprocity, support, and a willingness to lift each other up when someone is experiencing problems. Healthy families also foster a sense of safety and security in which family members can trust that vulnerabilities won't be exploited and that the family is a nurturing and warm place to land when life gets hard. Conflict is inevitable in any family, but when it happens in a healthy family, members are willing to work to resolve it.

A healthy family can acknowledge the changing roles as a daughter-in-law joins and a son shifts his priorities to his own family. Successful MIL-DIL relationships are created when there is mutuality and respect.[2] For example, when Tiffany and Andrew were moving into a new house around the holidays, his mother recognized that this was a major life event, and instead of demanding they accommodate her expectations on top of the stress of the move, she changed her holiday plans to work around their schedule. But if these dynamics are guided by fear and a need for control and power, the DIL can be left feeling like Allison: shut out.

In today's families, this negative treatment can feel especially egregious. Historically, DILs "married into" their husband's families, leaving their own behind. Many were expected to execute without complaint any chore their MIL required. But today, women who have experienced a higher level of equality in their workplaces and relationships may be surprised to find themselves up against what they see as outdated expectations. While we imagine that gendered expectations have changed significantly in North America, I often see women stymied by MILs who fully deferred to their own MIL only thirty or so years before and now expect the same from their own DIL.

The challenge is that younger generations of women know more and expect more. We expect basic autonomy and respect. And when our partners are struggling with long-standing interpersonal issues, we get curious about the legacies of their childhoods.

THE IMPACT OF TRAUMA

Allison realized that whenever she brought up William's mother, he would grow silent, find a diversion, and sidestep the conversation. In therapy, Allison connected his behavior to his mother being highly defensive and emotionally absent in the home while he was growing up. The origin of her problems was not mysterious. At three years old, Allison's MIL had been removed from her Indigenous family and separated from her siblings. The family that adopted her was stable but highly controlling and lacked emotional warmth. Allison began to understand that her MIL's approach to the family stemmed from trauma, both individual and generational.

Traumatic experiences can include addiction, child neglect, significant material losses, physical and emotional abuse, abandonment, significant health events, and so on. Of course, such experiences directly and negatively impact the individuals going through them. But people are also affected by trauma that they didn't personally live through. Clinicians use the term *generational trauma* to describe the passing down of traumatic experiences from one generation to the next, not only via behavior but also via biology. If, say, your grandparents were traumatized by living through a war, it might affect you by making them more emotionally absent than they would've been otherwise, but it also might show up in your very cells, even if the war happened before you were born. One study found that the behavioral impacts of early-life adversity in mice were passed down over three generations, suggesting that they were not learned but rather transmitted at a cellular level.[3]

When you join your husband's family, its individual and generational trauma histories may not be immediately apparent. Instead, you'll encounter family secrets, conversations that become heated and tense, or topics that are avoided altogether, as well as general unhealthy behaviors and maladaptive coping skills.

For example, when you choose to parent your children differently from the way your MIL parented hers, she might end up feeling confused, rejected, or less than. She might start to wonder if your choices imply that you think she was a bad mother, or worse, if they're proof she *was* a bad mother. But instead of being able to identify her emotions and tell herself that your parenting choices are not an indication that she was a defective mother, she might make passive-aggressive remarks that undermine you or refuse to follow your wishes regarding your kids. A more adaptive way of dealing with these feelings would be to notice the feeling of rejection, remind herself that she is worthy no matter what, and support your parenting choices. But if she doesn't have the ability to regulate her emotions, she'll end up displacing them and projecting them onto you and/or her son.

Acknowledging your MIL's history of trauma doesn't excuse her hurtful, confusing, or disrespectful behavior, but it can enhance your understanding and compassion. Instead of asking yourself, "Why is she like this?!" you can shift to "It makes sense that she does this." That simple shift can defuse a tremendous amount of tension and resentment.

That does not mean, however, that you need to make her aware of her own issues. As you learn about attachment styles, parenting, and cycle breaking, online or in books like this one, it can be tempting to try to pass this information on to your MIL. I like to remind my clients of these key factors to consider:

* Your MIL (or other people in your life, such as your parents) might not be ready to see their trauma or acknowledge the significant impact their history has on their present day.

* Most parents did the best that they could with the information they had.

* When it comes to generational trauma, no individual can completely overcome it. Instead, we each begin to change

the trajectory of behaviors and coping skills within ourselves and our families.

* We don't get to control others and their healing journeys.

* We are responsible for our own boundaries, not others'.

* Everyone is continuously growing and evolving. While someone might not be aware of their trauma history today, they might begin to build awareness at another time.

Looking at our families in this way can lead us to see the impact of trauma more clearly and change our responses to it for the better.

REPEATING CYCLES

Unlike trauma, behavioral cycles aren't necessarily created by big adverse life events; instead, they stem from the lessons we learn about how the world works, starting from our earliest interactions with caregivers. If our caregivers were warm and responsive, we learn it is normal to be warm and responsive. If our caregivers were dismissive and avoided conflict, we learn it is normal to dismiss others and avoid conflict.

These lessons begin long before we learn to talk or consciously reason. A child doesn't need to know the word *upset* to understand that their mother is upset; they are born with the ability to attune to the subtle changes on their caregiver's face. As their brain develops, this attunement helps guide their understanding of who they are, who others are, and how safe the world is. In a high-conflict home, a child's nervous system learns to be primed for potential danger.

As a result, when that child becomes an adult, they often end up repeating the patterns of behavior they grew up with. If they learned it was normal to solve problems calmly, they solve problems calmly. If they learned it was normal to yell a lot, they yell a lot. These patterns feel familiar and therefore comfortable to the brain, even when they're not helpful.

When Colin's stress level increased, he became highly critical of his wife. He'd point out every mistake, turn her complaints around on her, and criticize her parenting in front of the kids. Colin's behavior with his wife directly reflected his father's behavior with his mother. (Interestingly, Colin found a wife who struggled to set boundaries with him, just like his mother struggled to set boundaries with his father.) Colin was repeating a familiar cycle from his family of origin.

How do cycles repeat? They repeat out of a lack of awareness, or if there is awareness, out of uncertainty and fear of change. Colin wasn't thinking, "I really liked how my dad criticized my mom. I'm going to do the same thing with my wife." Instead, he's just doing what feels natural to him in the moment. Even if he wants to do something different, he doesn't know what that would look or feel like, so he ends up doing the same old thing he's used to. This is why, when you join a family system and you operate differently from that system, you are viewed as a threat. These repeating patterns feel safe and predictable; anything different feels weird and potentially dangerous, even if it's ultimately healthier.

You might seem especially threatening if one of the family patterns is codependency. Codependency is when one person in a relationship relies inappropriately on the other person with the expectation that the other person will sacrifice their emotional, mental, and physical needs in order to support them. In a codependent mother-child dynamic, the relationship revolves around the child tending to and prioritizing the mother's needs and wishes while neglecting their own. It's hard for the child to break out of this cycle, even if they grow to resent it, because they feel guilt about "abandoning" or "betraying" their mother.

A codependent mother-son relationship can sometimes be easy to identify, with the son being overly attentive to the mother.

More often, it's less obvious because many sons emotionally withdraw but physically capitulate. They may not seem particularly close with their mothers emotionally, but they continue to subordinate their needs to their mothers' by saying yes to requests they'd rather say no to or avoiding issues instead of dealing with them head-on. Until you arrived on the scene with a different perspective, your husband's family may have been unaware that any of this was in any way abnormal.

Given this lack of awareness, your spouse might fail to identify that anything needs to change. If this is something that your husband is expressing, the VAULT method's five steps will help you communicate what it is that you need, while also respecting his desire to protect and support his mother. That doesn't mean you'll be aiding in preserving toxic family dynamics. It means you'll be operating from a place of compassion for your husband while getting your own needs met.

CULTURE AND VALUES

When Abby said yes to her partner's proposal, she knew they would need to have important conversations before proceeding with their relationship. Abby, a third-generation Canadian, came from a different cultural background than her soon-to-be husband's, who had emigrated from India. His family, who still lived in India, had expectations of a wife that were unfamiliar to Abby, and together, she and her fiancé needed to decide what role those expectations would play in their relationship. It was not smooth sailing. While her husband intellectually knew he was marrying into a different culture, it was hard for him to let go of what he was raised with—and his mother had no interest in anything less than a "perfect" Indian wife for her son.

The culture we live in shapes our beliefs and attitudes, and we bring these beliefs and attitudes into our relationships. Yet couples frequently don't talk about their values or have conversations with their in-laws about what truly matters to them.

This can lead to conflict when one spouse doesn't share the cultural values and traditions the other spouse's parents assumed they would. This isn't the case only when spouses' families are from different countries; there can also be cultural gaps between different generations, religions, or even individual families (e.g., one partner's family discusses issues openly while the other thinks difficulties should be kept quiet). This is not to say one approach is necessarily better than another or that there aren't pros and cons to any given approach, just that partners from two different backgrounds will have to work to understand those differences.

Let's discuss some cultural differences that frequently contribute to conflict between mothers-in-law and daughters-in-law.

* **Collectivism vs. individualism:** Collectivist cultures focus on the needs of the group over those of the individual, in contrast with individualistic cultures, which do the opposite. If your family comes from one and your husband's family comes from the other, these conflicting goals will impact how you celebrate holidays, how you negotiate the time you spend with your in-laws, and the involvement of your MIL in your marriage. In some cultures, if a DIL chooses to prioritize her own family of origin, she is viewed as acting inappropriately, which leads to conflict with her in-law family.[4]

* **Avoidance vs. discussion:** Some cultures and value systems tend to discuss emotions more openly, while others believe that it's best not to talk about hard things. Some families believe that "giving time apart" will resolve issues, while others believe that any one member's issues are an entire family's conversation. These different approaches can make it hard to know how to handle conflict when it inevitably arises.

* **Family hierarchy:** Different cultures hold different views on who (if anyone) is prioritized or holds the authority in the family. In some, adult children are expected to obey their parents, put their family of origin first, and care for their elders. In some, a DIL is expected to enter into her in-law family and not interfere in the relationship between her husband and his family. In some, certain boundaries are seen as a violation of family bonds. These cultural beliefs are deeply rooted, hard to change, and can create conflict if you, the DIL, do not adhere to them.

* **The mother-son relationship:** In some cultures, the relationship between mother and son is expected to be extremely close and intense. For example, mothers may cry at their son's wedding not because they are overjoyed but because of their grief at "losing" their son. The term *mammismo* is used to describe the deep bond in Italian families between a man and his mother, which can damage the autonomy the son needs to maintain a healthy marriage.[5]

* **Gender roles:** Today, many couples are reevaluating previously accepted gender roles. Women, who often work outside the home, no longer want to be fully responsible for domestic labor, emotional labor, parenting, and "kin keeping" (maintaining family connections not only with your own family of origin but with your husband's too). However, if you approach these issues differently from your MIL, she may judge you or take it as a personal attack on her own choices.

Understanding how your cultural assumptions and values might clash with your MIL's can help you navigate those differences with less blame and more nuance.

TEN COMMON TOXIC FAMILY DYNAMICS

Most people don't intentionally set out to act in toxic ways. When people (like, perhaps, your mother-in-law) cling to toxic behavior, it's usually not because they're malicious but because they're trying to protect themselves from feelings of fear, pain, discomfort, and shame. Unlike guilt, which says, "I *did* something bad," shame says, "I *am* bad." Because shame threatens one's core sense of self so deeply, it can be a strong motivator to develop any defense mechanism against it, no matter how unhealthy.

It can be jarring, even "crazy making," to enter a family and see blatantly unhealthy patterns that no one else acknowledges. Some people lack the self-awareness required to see the problem, while others might simply be unwilling to face it. For many families, these long-standing patterns work well enough that they are tolerable; they prefer the predictability of the ongoing dysfunction to the unpredictable chaos they fear might ensue if they tried to change things. But that doesn't mean you must tolerate them.

My research and clinical work have led me to uncover ten common toxic family dynamics that tend to be in play when there are problems in the relationship between mother-in-law and daughter-in-law. These patterns are not mutually exclusive and tend to overlap with one another. You may notice some or all of them in your husband's family (or in your own family, for that matter). Let's explore these toxic behaviors in depth.

1. A CODEPENDENT ATTACHMENT BETWEEN MOTHER AND SON

A mother's codependent attachment to her son involves an inability to recognize that her son is not responsible for her emotional, mental, and physical well-being. While this mother struggles to identify and express her emotions, she implicitly or explicitly expects her son to self-sacrifice in order to meet her needs and focus on her wishes. She feels a sense of entitlement to her son's life and views her son's achievements as a reflection of her worth.

Challenges begin to arise when her son starts to build his own life emotionally and physically separate from his mother. Josh, after spending his formative years playing hockey competitively, decided to quit the sport and move across the country to the same city as his girlfriend. Hockey was his parents' dream, but he had other desires for his life. When he told his mother, her first response was "Did you even think of the impact this would have on us?," which led Josh to feel guilt and shame for wanting his own life. Josh felt that it was his responsibility to keep his mother happy, even if it made him unhappy.

In a codependent relationship, there are few to no boundaries, which are seen as barriers to intimacy or threats to the "oneness" of a close relationship. But the truth is that boundaries are essential to healthy family dynamics. Instead of building walls, they help to build bridges. But the mother who struggles to stay connected in an adaptive way has challenges accepting her adult child's limits, wants, and needs. She struggles to respect her son's autonomy when he says no.

A lack of boundaries in families leads to enmeshment, the dynamic in which everyone in the family system is obligated to think and feel the same thing. If a mother is upset, her son is supposed to be upset too—and if he doesn't arrive there on his own, he'll be pressured into it. My client Talia struggled with an MIL so enmeshed with her son that she expected to have a say in what clothes he wore, how they decorated their home, and how they parented their children. Talia's MIL would also show up unannounced at their house, even after Talia's husband told her not to come over without texting first, because in her mind, if she wanted to visit her son, he must also want to visit her.

Enmeshed families believe that "more time together is better," valuing quantity of time over quality of connection—even though research of newlyweds has found that more contact in general with in-laws doesn't necessarily lead to a better relationship and that the quality of the relationship improves when it is not forced or coerced.[6]

2. HIGH LEVELS OF RIGIDITY AND CONTROL

People who come from chaotic upbringings often develop a high need for control. They feel, consciously or not, that controlling the people around them will keep the family safe. Excessively rigid parents are resistant to change, hold unreasonable rules, and enforce a strong family hierarchy in who makes decisions. If your MIL is like this, she might be inflexible, have unrealistically high expectations, and insist on being right. Research shows that in a highly rigid family, adolescents experience their parents as more disengaged in their life, suggesting that rigidity isn't about building interconnectedness but instead is about upholding a certain family structure.[7]

Elijah grew up in a family that had run a business for several generations, and everyone colluded in prioritizing the needs of the business over the emotional needs of family members. His parents quashed any attempts to assert independence or autonomy. When Elijah decided not to return home after college and to seek his own identity and career, his parents characterized it as a betrayal of them and the family. His wife married into a dynamic where she and her husband were always treated as outsiders and traitors, even as her in-laws were constantly trying to bring her husband back under their heel. There was no flexibility in letting people determine their own paths; everyone had to submit to parental control or be punished.

3. MANIPULATION AND GUILT TRIPS

The MIL who uses manipulation and guilt trips wants power over other people. When her kids assert their boundaries, she tries to get around them with comments like "I guess you don't have any time for me anymore" and "We'll be all by ourselves this holiday if you don't come." The goal is to impose a feeling of guilt on you through passive-aggressive statements, nonverbal cues, silent treatments, or the suggestion that you owe her. I've noticed that when people grow up on the receiving end of this behavior, they struggle to accurately identify it as manipulative. Instead, they become desensitized to it and characterize it as "just Mom."

While Maribel was on maternity leave with her first daughter, her MIL abruptly decided to take early retirement and requested her son and his family attend her retirement ceremony, a six-hour flight away from where they lived. Maribel was not excited about making the trip with a newborn, but she was equally unexcited about being left alone for seventy-two hours while her husband, Leo, went without her. She suspected her MIL was doing this to take the family's focus away from Maribel and the baby and put it back on herself. When Leo tried to convey that Maribel's absence wasn't a slight, his mother would cry and tell him he didn't care about her anymore. He felt enormously manipulated and unsupported as he was navigating life with a new baby. In the end, he got on the plane, but it was the beginning of a new period of renegotiation.

4. EXCLUSION OF "OUTSIDERS"

Families who are enmeshed end up creating a sense of group-think. "This is how *we* do things" is the family motto, without any consideration that other ways to do things might work just as well (or better). They find it hard to integrate an "outsider" like a daughter-in-law into their group, especially when the DIL is not "like us." Instead of extending herself to see her DIL's perspective, the MIL worries her son and his wife will exclude her and views the DIL as a threat to the family system.[8] There is an "us versus you" paradigm that often makes the DIL out to be the "bad guy" or scapegoat. Any disruption to the family's previous routine is blamed on the DIL.

Haley grew up in the same small town as her husband, but even so, she was always made to feel like an outsider at her husband's family events. Her offers to pitch in were rebuffed. Dishes she cooked would go uneaten. When she engaged in conversation with her MIL or shared different ways to view a situation, she would be met with dismissal and rejection.

5. TRIANGULATION

The term *triangulation* describes a dynamic in which a third person is brought into a relationship between two other people in order to alleviate tension. Maybe your mother-in-law texts you to ask why her son is being stubborn, putting you in the middle of the conflict instead of talking to him directly. Or, conversely, maybe she keeps bringing her problems with you to her son, inserting herself in your marriage dynamic as a source of conflict. I find there are also some MILs who talk to their DILs about other family members (the father-in-law, the husband's siblings, etc.), and while these disclosures might be seen as efforts to create connection, research shows they can negatively impact the MIL-DIL relationship.[9]

Your husband might be the one engaging in triangulation as well. June's eldest son had a blood disorder that required careful management and occasionally necessitated a trip to the ER. When these crises arose, June realized her husband had a habit of giving his mother minimal information about the situation and then going silent. Out of anxiety and stress, her MIL would want to know more, but since her son had stopped responding, she'd text and call June. June, wanting to be compassionate and kind, would return her frantic texts and phone calls, but that meant she was distracted by managing her MIL's anxiety when she needed to stay focused on her own son and his health emergency. Over time, as her husband wasn't setting clear boundaries with his mother about sharing information, and June wasn't asserting her own boundaries with her husband or MIL, June began to grow resentful toward her MIL *and* her husband.

Another type of triangle that happens in toxic family systems is the *drama triangle*. According to Dr. Stephen Karpman, there are three roles that make up the drama triangle: the victim, the persecutor, and the rescuer.[10]

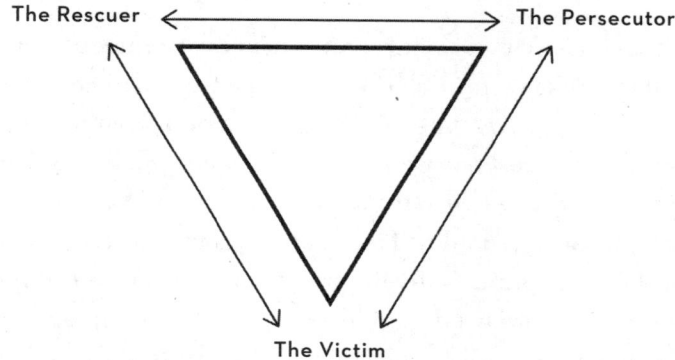

The Rescuer ⟵⟶ The Persecutor

The Victim

The victim feels helpless, powerless, ashamed, and unable to solve their problems or make active changes. They often play the "poor me" role in the family. The persecutor is more righteous, controlling, and critical. They are angry and rigid, often saying, "It's all your fault" or "I told you so." Finally, the rescuer steps in to help and smooth things over, enabling the dynamic to continue because the root of the conflict between the victim and the persecutor is never truly addressed. The rescuer's actions help keep the victim stuck and dependent, leading them to believe they cannot solve their own problems.

Renee and her husband, Neil, were going to take a day trip with the kids out to the lake, but an hour before they planned to leave, his mother called in a panic to tell him that her washing machine had flooded. Neil asked his mother to get his father to participate in cleaning up, but his father refused, saying, "I told your mother not to trust those contractors." Neil felt obligated to go help his mother, so Renee and the kids ended up taking the family trip alone. They all fell into their previous roles: Neil's mother played the victim, his father played the persecutor, and Neil was the rescuer in the middle of the drama triangle.

6. ADULT CHILD AS FAMILY EMOTIONAL REGULATOR

In a home where emotional safety isn't consistently present, children learn that certain feelings and needs aren't acceptable and develop alternative strategies to remain connected to their caregivers. As I once heard child psychologist Dr. Becky Kennedy say at an event, when parents don't repair, kids turn to either self-blame or self-doubt. They believe they themselves are the cause of their parents' feelings; if their parents are happy, it's because they were good, and if their parents are unhappy, it's because they were bad. If your husband's childhood was like this, he may have learned it was his job to push away his own feelings and needs in order to soothe his parents—and his parents may have unconsciously learned that was his job as well. As an adult, he still feels overly responsible for managing his mother's feelings.

Carlos's mother was depressed throughout his childhood. He recalled times of sitting at her bedside and sharing only positive things from the day. When, as kids do, he tried to share hard moments, like getting rejected by his friend or not getting picked for a sports team, she would tell him not to upset her with these kinds of stories. Today, Carlos expects his wife to join him in emotionally supporting his mother's needs above her own needs and those of their small children.

7. TAKING THINGS PERSONALLY

Building a healthy sense of self requires the ability to differentiate, to understand that two people can have separate ways of viewing and understanding the world—and that disagreement isn't inherently a personal attack. However, in families that struggle to build healthy interconnectedness, people take others' actions and choices personally. If you do things differently from the way your MIL prefers, she may feel that you're attacking her, even if you don't actually intend any criticism.

Ian and Astra made the decision to move to a different city to be closer to Astra's workplace and minimize her commute. While they still lived within an hour's drive of Ian's mom, she took the move personally and felt that they made the decision to spite her. Although they reassured her that they made the move for their own family's needs and that they would continue to see her frequently, his mother remained upset and didn't speak to them for weeks. Today, she continues to make passive-aggressive remarks about them abandoning her.

8. A HISTORY OF PHYSICAL DISCIPLINE/ABUSE

While hitting children was once considered a normal form of discipline, studies continue to show that it creates a lack of physical and emotional safety in a way that is damaging to a child's sense of self.[11] From a psychological and relational perspective, physical abuse teaches children to fear connection with others rather than to show up authentically, make mistakes, and learn to build compassion. Some children who experienced physical abuse will create more distance from their family members as adults, while others will normalize the experience, saying it was just how parenting was at the time and that they "turned out fine."

As a child, Caleb and his brothers were regularly spanked for "breaking the rules." In fact, his mother would joke about spinning her spiky engagement ring around to her palm when she "really needed to make a point." Today, Caleb has trouble authentically connecting to his mother, who has never apologized, and yet he desperately seeks her approval. Now that he has become a father, addressing this legacy has taken on greater urgency for him and his wife.

9. REFUSAL TO TAKE RESPONSIBILITY

The foundation of a healthy relationship is the ability to take ownership of the mistakes we make and the impact we have on others. People who struggle with this exhibit a personality trait called the tendency for interpersonal victimhood (TIV), characterized by a high need for recognition, moral elitism, limited empathy for others, and a tendency to get stuck in rumination.[12] They also tend toward negative cognitive biases and unstable self-esteem. All of this makes it particularly difficult for them to see or take responsibility for the role they might be playing in a given problem.

Silvia made efforts to build a relationship with her MIL, yet her MIL would frequently ignore her at family events and exclude her from conversations. Interestingly, Silvia and her husband lived next door to his family, adding an extra layer of complexity to their relationship. When Silvia's husband tried to speak to his mother about her behavior, she grew defensive and deflected any possible acknowledgment that she contributed to the relationship challenges.

10. PARENTIFICATION

It's not the role of a child, especially when they're still young, to listen to a parent complain about the other parent, be leaned upon for advice, or be expected to solve a parent's issues. Yet in some families, a child is parentified and expected to take on adult situations like making meals, caring for other siblings, or putting away their emotions in order to look after and care for their parents.

Even when children are adults, it isn't their job to act as therapist or marital mediator. But if your husband has what psychologist Dr. Lindsay Gibson calls "emotionally immature parents," they may continue to act as if the point of his life is taking care of their needs while forgoing his own.[13] These are parents who reject their adult child's feelings, seek attention, turn every conversation back to themselves, and/or are emotionally absent.

Anton called his parents nightly to check in on them on top of seeing them once a week. Over time, he began to realize that every conversation focused on a minor problem that his mother had blown out of proportion into a huge crisis. If he tried to talk about his struggles at work or discuss his hobbies, his mom would turn the conversation back to her own problems. Anton began to see that his parents didn't have a genuine interest in deeply knowing him.

Exercise:
Questions to Ask About Your Partner's Family

If your partner doesn't have much insight into the dynamics in his family, this is entirely normal. Most sons—most people—don't intentionally ignore or condone their family's unhealthy behavior. They're simply desensitized to it. But even without your partner's participation, you will likely find it helpful to consider the following questions about his family:

* What role does each member of the family play?

* Who makes decisions in the family?

* What happens if one or both of his parents don't get what they want?

* What do his parents do with their own emotions?

* How are disappointments communicated and dealt with?

* Does one family member play a key role in navigating the emotions of others? What do they do or not do?

* What does your husband do during visits in response to negative comments or unhelpful behavior from his mother?

FAMILY PATTERNS: DISRUPTED OR CONSTANT?

Allison and William, whom we met at the beginning of the chapter, began to feel more like a team once Allison started to understand the dynamics of the family she'd entered into. She understood her Good Girl tendencies, but she also came to understand that her MIL was a Victim type and constantly pulled for a codependent relationship with William. William's mother had never learned to communicate her own needs clearly and could only express them passive-aggressively. Identifying this history helped Allison build compassion for her MIL while also recognizing that she was not responsible for healing William's family's deep-rooted wounds. Allison was also able to see the enmeshment in his family: Her MIL thought William was still an extension of her and should have the same thoughts and feelings as she had.

Eventually, Allison came to accept a powerful truth: She had joined a family with enmeshment and codependency issues, and she was never going to be able to fix that on her own. Instead of trying to tend to her MIL's feelings by being a Good Girl, she started pouring effort into her own self-worth and identity so she could show up in the relationship with more confidence and better boundaries.

While it can feel uncomfortable to push back against entrenched dynamics, acknowledging family patterns and the very real difficulty in altering these patterns is essential. It's important for you to know that deciding to approach them differently doesn't mean you're doing something bad. Rather, it indicates that something needed to change for you and your husband to have a positive relationship while also finding a way to coexist alongside your MIL. Your job isn't to change their pattern but to find a way to make the relationship work for you.

The challenges you have with your MIL didn't start with you. There is a history, a context, and a system that has been operating since long before you joined the family. This recognition can help you to depersonalize your MIL's actions and behaviors. It was never about you but about the potential change you represented to the system that was already there, a system that wasn't necessarily healthy. Now that you understand the system you're operating in, it's time to examine how your actions might be contributing to problems in your relationship with your mother-in-law so that you can start to do something different.

Chapter 3

ADDRESSING OUR OWN BAGGAGE

---

*E*ver since Cassandra and Michael's wedding, her friends had been talking about how lucky Cassandra was in the mother-in-law department. She had a built-in babysitter just down the street, her fridge was never empty of lasagna, and every time one of her friends met her MIL, they felt they were being taken care of by this warm Italian mother figure. But that was not how Cassandra felt.

Of course, it was nice to have support, but Cassandra's MIL seemed to believe this support entitled her to do whatever she wanted whenever she wanted. When she wanted to see the kids, she simply came over, often unannounced. She even showed up unannounced at the hospital after Cassandra gave birth, saying, "It's nothing I haven't seen before, hon," and grabbing "her bambino" out of Cassandra's hands. While Michael tried to be empathetic, he ultimately didn't see any issues. His response was often "But she's helping" or "She cares for us." But Cassandra didn't feel cared for. She felt controlled. She needed her own fridge space for the food she wanted to cook for her family— which wasn't pasta seven nights a week. She wanted a weekend with just her husband and her kids, without having to host her MIL at a moment's notice.

The situation reached a boiling point when Cassandra's youngest needed emergency surgery. Over the two weeks that their grandson was hospitalized, Cassandra's in-laws texted looking for updates but never once visited the ICU or put in any of the caring that Cassandra and Michael needed. Michael kept making excuses for his mother's behavior. Cassandra knew she needed to make a change, but she felt completely unable to do so.

Why? Cassandra's early childhood consisted of learning to stay quiet around an alcoholic father who was physically abusive. A word spoken out of turn, and she would be hit. She quickly learned to avoid her father's wrath either by placating him and being the good girl or by retreating to her room to hide from his angry outbursts. Her mother encouraged her to "be good" so as not to set her father off. Having grown up in an environment where her needs were considered unimportant and asserting herself was impossible, she didn't know how to communicate her needs or assert herself with her MIL.

When Cassandra showed up to my office, she could clearly see the dysfunction in her husband's family of origin. What was less obvious to her was how her old family patterns were playing out and how parts of her behavior were contributing to the problems she was experiencing. It was time to claim her baggage.

GETTING CURIOUS

The first step in the process of addressing your own baggage is simply getting curious about how your formative experiences might be influencing how you're experiencing your current situation. Take some time to reflect on the following questions:

* What role do I currently play or have I previously played in my family of origin?

* How did each of my parents deal with their own in-laws?

* What type of expectations or relationship dynamics did I see unfolding between my parents and their in-laws? (E.g.: What did your family do at holidays? What unwritten rules guided their actions?)

* How was conflict handled in my family?

* What experiences have I had with authority figures?

* What are/were my expectations of my MIL, especially in the early days of dating and marrying my husband?

* What is/was my husband's expectation of the relationship between me and his mother?

We're going to start this exploration by first looking at the inner wounds that might stem from your earliest relationships and experiences. This will help you see how old unmet needs and coping mechanisms show up in your relationship with your MIL. We'll then explore your expectations, assumptions, and interpretations of your MIL, which will allow you to see how some of your unspoken thought processes might be contributing to the current situation. We'll then identify the unconscious patterns in your relationships that may lead to unresolved conflict.

As you begin to develop more awareness of how your history might be in play, I encourage you to extend grace and compassion to both yourself *and* your partner. Through this process, you'll see that you have more control than you previously thought. You will become empowered to feel and operate differently, so that you and your husband can build a working relationship with your MIL.

MEETING YOUR INNER CHILD

The messages you receive from caregivers about yourself, other people, and the world during your formative years become driving forces in how you experience and make sense of your life, unconsciously impacting what you do as an adult. While some clinicians discuss this in terms of "parts" in an "internal family system," I like to refer to the "inner child."

We all have an inner child that represents the younger part of us. If we didn't get our needs met in our early years or were told hurtful and untrue things about ourselves directly or indirectly, our inner child can be wounded. While it's often unproductive to blame our parents for not being able to give us what we needed, we can acknowledge that there was a mismatch between our longings and the environment that we grew up in. Our parents likely did the best they could with what they had, *and* we still had needs that were not met.

When you feel like you become irrational, do things on autopilot, or are no longer speaking from the logical part of your brain, it's a sign that your inner child has taken over. If you don't bring awareness and healing to your inner child, she will continue to carry these wounds forward. But the good news is that once you identify your inner child and know when she shows up, you can start meeting your own needs and acting with intentionality. Why does this matter when it comes to dealing with your husband and his mother? Because it's likely that, in both of these relationships, there is a younger part of you that is still looking for attention and validation. But the ways you're trying to get these needs met might be creating more tension and working against your goals.

I developed the following ten inner child types based on my nearly two decades of clinical experience. You might identify with one or more of these; you may also see your husband's inner child in these types. Each type is defined by how they would finish this sentence: "In order to be loved, seen, and accepted, I need to . . ."

* **The Good Kid:** *"I need to be good."* Your inner child fears rejection and disappointment, and so to feel loved, you try to be obliging and nice. You seek acceptance by not letting others down. Your core coping mechanism is to strive for agreeability and compliance, minimizing and ignoring your own desires.

* **The People Pleaser:** *"I need to subjugate myself."* Rather than actively trying to be good, you passively give up your autonomy and desires in service of pleasing others. You learned to put others' needs first, which ultimately allowed you not to feel abandoned when your own needs were rejected. You likely learned that your needs are a burden. Your core coping mechanism is to self-sacrifice, making it difficult to identify and assert your own boundaries and needs.

* **The Golden Child:** *"I need to achieve perfection."* Your inner child thrives on overachieving and doing things the "right way" as defined by others. You experienced love and validation only for what you did, not for who you are. Consequently, you continue to feel like you need to excel and stand out. Your core coping mechanism is to strive and overfunction.

* **The Micromanager:** *"I need predictability and control."* To stay safely connected with others and get your needs met, you require rigid routine and boundaries. You likely experienced instability or unpredictability as a child, which led you to believe that if you can control things, you will feel safe and soothed. Your core coping mechanism is to

maintain orderliness, which likely results in conflict when others want the autonomy to make their own decisions.

* **The Caregiver:** *"I need to care for everyone."* Your inner child learned that when you catered to everyone else's needs first, you were seen and given attention. You learned to help others and solve their problems, ensuring connection. Although you feel close to others, this closeness is one-sided, as you're aware of the other person's needs but you don't make them aware of yours. Today, you fear not being needed, so you insert yourself in others' difficulties. You likely also experience resentment in your relationships due to overextending yourself and having porous boundaries. Your core coping mechanism is to focus on the desires of everyone else.

* **The Rebel:** *"I need to rebel against authority."* Your caregiver used their authority to exert control over you. Since this was your earliest experience of being close with someone, you now fear that getting close to anyone means they'll try to control you as well. Today, you struggle against rules and being told what to do, especially if it feels like it's coming from an authoritarian approach. Your core coping mechanism is to fight against others, which allows you to stay distant from them.

* **The Wallflower:** *"I need to blend in, be quiet, and stay small."* Your inner child doubts yourself and your abilities, so you follow others and let them take the lead. You play small to avoid risking judgment, criticism, or abandonment. Because of self-doubt, your core coping mechanism is to look to others' opinions and not trust your own.

* **The Obedient:** *"I need to honor my parent(s)."* Your inner child is bound by loyalty and defers unquestioningly to

authority. You fear losing love if you don't follow your parent's model of how to live. Your core coping mechanism is to align your choices with those of your parent, which makes it difficult in your marriage as you struggle to choose between obeying your parent or pursuing unity with your spouse.

* **The Joker:** *"I need to be the class clown."* You learned that to be seen and loved, you needed to be happy, easygoing, and entertaining. You received praise for alleviating conflict through humor, and you were likely punished for normal, non-happy emotional reactions. Your core coping mechanism is to create emotional distance by making light of situations and not asserting your needs.

* **The Self-Protector:** *"I need to protect myself."* In your early life, being vulnerable led to pain, rejection, or abandonment, and therefore, your inner child learned that trusting others is unsafe. Your core coping mechanism is creating emotional walls, withdrawing, and keeping loved ones at a distance.

When Cassandra started to explore her experiences as a child in our therapy sessions, she found herself repeatedly coming back to her desire to be a good girl and never assert her needs. This made sense as a strategy to avoid her father's rage as a child, but as an adult, she was filled with self-doubt and defaulted to letting others make decisions for her, including in her career and with her closest friends. When she began to ask her inner child what she needed, she found herself feeling fears of being abandoned or punished for having normal emotions. It was helpful for her to be reminded that as an adult today, she could now meet her own needs.

As she began to get more in touch with her emotions and the anger she felt toward her MIL, Cassandra initially became more reactive and defensive with both her husband and her MIL. This isn't unexpected when someone starts to label their feelings and tune into their needs, but it did indicate that there was more work we needed to do. One session, she recalled "talking back" to her MIL and expressed the shame she felt for "acting out of turn." I reframed this moment as her inner child taking over, a wounded part of her both having a meltdown and trying to protect herself. I invited her to offer compassionate words to her inner child, but Cassandra didn't know what to say. In my therapist role, I took over, looking over my shoulder as if to imagine that little Cassandra was standing behind us. "Hey, little Cassie," I said, "you're safe. I see you, and I've got you." Cassandra burst into tears, seeing that, as an adult, she didn't have to be so afraid.

YOUR EXPECTATIONS

We all enter relationships with expectations of how things will go, and our relationships with our in-laws are no exception. If your family of origin is warm, caring, and connected, perhaps you hope or expect your husband's family will be similar. Or maybe you long to be close to your mother-in-law because your own mother was narcissistic, emotionally immature, or absent. Either way, your expectations will impact your relationship with your MIL.

Where do these expectations come from? They can stem from what we saw watching our own parents' relationships with their in-laws. If you saw your parents navigate conflict well, you'll likely believe that you and your in-laws can work through difficulties. If your mother spoke negatively of her MIL, you might have negative expectations of how your MIL will act. Our beliefs about our MILs are also influenced by our experiences with other female authority figures like mentors or teachers. Were older women in your life supportive and collaborative? Or were they passive-aggressive and authoritarian? How you see yourself in relation to older women based on these past experiences will also lead you to form specific narratives of your MIL. Expectations also come from socialization, from cultural and religious beliefs, and even from the media, which often portrays MILs as conflictual figures (e.g., Raymond's mother on *Everybody Loves Raymond* or Jane Fonda's role in *Monster-in-Law*). It makes sense to have built up ideals of what this relationship should look like.

Underneath these experiences, our expectations come from a core place of either fear or desire. For example, if you're coming from a place of fear, you might expect that your partner will prioritize his mother's needs and wishes over yours, leading to expectations like "A mother-in-law won't be supportive of a daughter-in-law" or "He'll always choose his mother over me." Such expectations aim to protect us from the possibility that we could be abandoned or rejected, especially if we had negative experiences in our own families. Our unconscious narratives tell us that if we expect pain, sadness, and loss, they won't hurt as much when they inevitably arrive. But fear-based expectations can't protect us from pain; in fact, they can actually enhance feelings of resentment and disappointment.

If, on the other hand, our expectations come from a place of desire, they can indicate what we're missing and what we need. Instead of focusing on what you want to avoid (like abandonment and rejection), they focus on what you want to create. Connection, mutuality, trust, respect—all of these are appropriate desires for your relationship with your MIL and your husband. At the same time, you don't get to choose your MIL. If you desire a best friend or a mother figure, and your MIL simply isn't that person, you might have to grieve the loss of those hoped-for expectations. But overall, we're more likely to build the relationships we want when we set our expectations based on desire rather than fear.

Why? If you hold negative expectations of your MIL, especially if they stem from a place of fear, they might become a self-fulfilling prophecy. When we expect a certain outcome, we can subconsciously act in ways that lead us to experience that outcome. Research has found that those with negative expectations of their MIL before their wedding were indeed more likely to have a negative relationship with their MIL after the wedding.[1] If you expect your MIL to be controlling, you might experience her advice as controlling, even if that's not her intention. It can be helpful to ask yourself, "What is driving my expectation? Is this fear? Or is it a need that I can communicate?"

However, it's also true that the bigger the difference between our expectation and reality, the more likely we are to struggle, so if we don't check our desire-based expectations, we may start to feel frustrated or resentful. You might expect your MIL to be genuinely interested in you as a person but find that she only asks about your baby's sleep schedule. You might expect everyone to consider each other's wishes while planning family holidays, but instead, your MIL unilaterally sets the schedule. If these expectations can't be met, then there is work to be done to grieve the idea of the relationship you wanted. This is as true with an MIL as it might be with your own parent. To move on and productively address what *is*, we must first grieve what we never received.

While grieving a hoped-for relationship with your MIL is part of your work, I reject the notion that we can set our expectations "too high" when it comes to how we're treated. You should have high expectations for how people treat you. You should expect people to treat you with respect, compassion, and consideration. Research shows that when partners have higher expectations going into a relationship, they are more likely to find a partner who matches their level of respect, trust, and mutuality.[2] So while we don't want to hold unrealistic expectations, we should also never tolerate unacceptable behaviors. In navigating your relationship with your MIL, you are allowed to expect to be treated respectfully.

YOUR ASSUMPTIONS
AND INTERPRETATIONS

In addition to expectations, we all hold assumptions and interpretations of other people and their behavior, and these play a role in how you perceive your MIL's actions. Assumptions are the guesses you make about how people will act and how situations will unfold based on your past experiences, your values, and your emotional reactions. They're mental shortcuts in our brains that help us understand our experiences. Assumptions can be neutral or positive, but too often, they become negative filters.

As a therapist, even though I know we all hold assumptions, I was surprised to see my son start making negative assumptions as early as age six. I often found myself entering cognitive therapist mode when he, for instance, assumed a friend wouldn't be available for a playdate. I'd say things like "That's an interesting thought; let's test that out" or "That's one way to look at it, but I imagine there are other ways too."

Our assumptions contribute to our interpretations—that is, the way we attach meaning to someone's actions. Interpretations are more conscious than assumptions, actively asking: Am I understanding your behavior as positive with good intentions, or am I understanding your behavior as negative with the intent to criticize, insult, or harm? This is important because the way you interpret your MIL's behavior plays a large role in how you're going to feel toward her and what happens in your relationship. Research suggests that if you view your MIL's actions and comments as negative or critical of who you are as a person, you're more likely to have a negative relationship with her.[3] But if you view what your MIL is doing as positive or unrelated to who you are as a person, you're likely to have a more respectful relationship with her.

To challenge your assumptions, it can be helpful to ask one simple question: Is this a fact, or is this a story I tell myself?

Then ask yourself: How do I *want* to understand my MIL's behavior, and is it more beneficial for everyone if I don't assume it's negative or interpret it as critical of me?

As one client told me, as a child she was compelled to "share everything" with her mother, who was boundaryless and intrusive. Now, as a married adult, she interpreted her MIL's questions about her life and offers of emotional support as threats to her autonomy and violations of her privacy, even though she eventually realized that was not how her MIL meant those things. If she hadn't assumed her MIL was acting with ill intent, certain conflicts might have been avoided.

In some cases, your relationship with your MIL might be so charged with conflict and tension that you perceive all types of messages as hurtful rather than being able to distinguish nuances in communication.[4] While you can't change your MIL, you can begin to see some of her behavior in a different light. So ask yourself if you're holding on to any assumptions or interpretations that you could put down.

WE REPEAT WHAT WE DON'T REPAIR

Here is a truth that many people struggle to see: We repeat what we don't repair. That is, we reenact what was originally done to us by our caregivers, continuing patterns from childhood in a way that stops us from getting what we need in our relationships today. While this can sometimes feel hard to acknowledge, I want you to know that we all do this in some way and that many of my clients come into therapy thinking this isn't the case, only to discover that they are in fact playing out their own familiar patterns.

If your inner child has unhealed wounds, you will most likely end up doing one of three things in your relationships:

1. **You do to your partner what your parent once did to you.** If your parents treated you with hostility or rage, for example, you might do the same to your husband during conflicts. My client Zoey would shout and slam doors like her father had as she told her husband how upset she was about his mother's guilt trips. But her husband couldn't see what kind of support she really needed because all he saw was her anger, which only pushed him further away.

2. **You elicit the same responses from your partner that you received from your parent.** If your parents were defensive or didn't consider your needs important, today you might behave in ways that lead your husband to respond the same way. This was the case for Iris, who experienced her parents dismissing her needs as unimportant, often saying, "Well, I guess we just can't get anything right with you." Now Iris lists all the things her husband has done wrong until he finally says, "Well, I guess I just can't get anything right with you."

3. **You do to yourself what your parents did to you.** If your parents shamed you for having needs, you might end up suppressing your own healthy needs for security and connection—often unbeknownst to your husband. Every time Naomi wanted to speak up about her MIL's criticisms of her weight, she would talk herself out of it, telling herself that she was being too sensitive. By silencing herself, she was unwittingly reenacting the same damaging dynamic she had endured as a child.

Why do we engage in these familiar strategies? Because they make our relationships feel more familiar, and familiarity feels "safe," even when it's not functional or working for us in the long run.

These processes of reenactment give meaning to the expression "We repeat what we don't repair." You're not just repeating the same fight over and over again with your husband or MIL, you're also repeating experiences of childhood that you have not yet processed or built effective coping mechanisms for. You're trying to get your needs met, but ultimately these patterns work against you. If you can identify this dynamic, you can start to change it.

HEALING YOUR INNER CHILD AND BREAKING PATTERNS

Even if old wounds are affecting your current life, you can start healing your inner child and break out of old patterns that aren't getting your needs met. By simply recognizing what your inner child sounds like, you can begin working toward something different.

Here are strategies to help you move forward in this work:

1. **Label the roles you played.** Your sense of agency will come from identifying your roles in your family. What did you do to try to stay connected and secure with your parents? Today, what do you do to get your needs met in your marriage? (Are you self-critical? Are you critical of your partner?) What experiences did you have with authority figures, and how might those play a role today?

2. **Identify and recognize unmet needs.** Learning the situations that trigger your inner child's wounds are important. On your phone or in a journal, jot down when you notice your inner child showing up. What need did you have in that moment that wasn't being met?

3. **Practice validation and compassion.** Many people end up getting critical of themselves when they experience challenges. This self-criticism ends up keeping you stuck in a loop of self-doubt and self-blame. Instead, practice providing empathy and validation for the emotions you

feel. Self-compassion allows you to see the common humanity in what you experience while also being kind to yourself, the same way you would to a dear friend.

4. **Imagine your younger self.** Using an old photo of you or imagining yourself at a younger age, see if you can focus on the face of your younger self. When doing this, ask what she needs or what she wishes other people understood. (For a list of eight core relational needs, you can refer to pages 79–83.)

5. **Practice reframing unhelpful beliefs.** Your inner child holds outdated beliefs related to her sense of self. They often sound like "if-then" statements, such as "If I am perfect, then I will be loved," "If I don't state my needs, then I will be accepted," or "If I stay quiet, then I won't be rejected." These beliefs lead you to understand acceptance and worthiness as conditional. Start from a place of worthiness and knowing that you are enough. Practice identifying the things that make up your identity that are unconditional. To be loved and accepted does not mean that you have to meet a certain standard or condition.

6. **Reparent yourself.** Give yourself what you wish you could have received as a child. Build reassuring statements you can repeat to yourself and practice seeing all your emotions as okay. Give yourself what you need through small moments of self-care throughout the day and exercise prioritizing your boundaries.

YOU'RE ALLOWED TO CHANGE

Cassandra came to see that before she could repair her relationship with her mother-in-law, she had to do some healing work on her own. Remember, she had grown up with an alcoholic, physically abusive father. In dealing with her MIL, she was operating from the messaging that she received from her mother: Be good and accept things as they are, or the consequences will be severe. Once she recognized these old patterns, we focused on creating healthy communication strategies to help her husband understand what she was struggling with. Cassandra then came to peace with being the one to set boundaries, stepping into her adult voice without fear instead of leaning on her husband to change the situation. It wasn't easy, but over time, change happened.

Sometimes we have trouble giving ourselves permission to change, so let me say: You are allowed to change. You are allowed to decide that something you did for your MIL in the past no longer works for you today. You are allowed to create new boundaries with your MIL, even if things have been the same for many years. You are allowed to be a different version of yourself. Perhaps it once served you to lean into a certain role when you were trying to find your footing in a new relationship and family dynamic. But if it doesn't connect to your values and you realize it doesn't serve you anymore, you get to change. This is true in any area of your life; if you once valued high control with your children (e.g., tightly scheduled bedtime routines, strict rules about specific foods), but now they're getting older and you'd like to change course, do so. You don't need to let old narratives of yourself continue to dictate what you do today—even if something was "working" for you before. And if it was never really working, that's even more reason to discover what is important to you today.

As you start to change, your new behavior will ask those around you to wake up too. You will meet their actions or comments differently, which will push them to either accept that you're different or resist and experience more tension. When one person in a dynamic changes, there is an opportunity for the whole dynamic to change.

In Cassandra's case, her MIL was initially upset about these new boundaries, as anyone might be. She was used to doing whatever she wanted with no pushback. But she adjusted alongside the family, and while there was more distance than what she was initially used to, over time, she was eventually able to offer support in a way that respected Cassandra's boundaries.

Giving time for change to happen is not bad. Things may not be resolved quickly, but that doesn't mean the whole situation will unravel. Change requires teaching ourselves new habits, and any habit requires repetition before it becomes second nature. This takes time for everyone involved, and that's okay. Healthy relationships are built on coming together and then having time apart for self-reflection and opportunities to build self-awareness. This balance between the needs of the individual and the needs of the relationship is something we'll explore in depth in the next chapter.

Chapter 4

FROM
"YOU VERSUS ME"
TO "WE"

Sasha and her husband, Nikhil, hadn't spoken to each other for two days when they showed up at my office. It's not uncommon for couples to arrive in the midst of giving each other the silent treatment following an explosive argument. In this case, they'd been having a routine fight over the division of labor and who was doing what in the household. But there was an additional challenge: Nikhil's mother had recently moved in with them.

In previous sessions, we had explored the impact of this cohabitation on their relationship as a couple and on their individual relationships with Nikhil's mother. Sasha had complained about her mother-in-law not respecting her requests and Nikhil not standing up for her, leaving her feeling like a dismissed outsider in her own home. Through our work, it had become clear that Nikhil's mother viewed him as "the golden child" and could see no fault in him.

In this fight about how the house was being cleaned, Sasha accused Nikhil of barely contributing to domestic chores at all, and Nikhil repeatedly deflected with "You're too demanding." Sasha thought she could seek help from her MIL. She knocked on her MIL's bedroom door, tears streaming down her face, and said, "He's your son. Can't you help him see this?"

It's common and natural for one woman to look to the other woman in the household for nurturance, empathy, and compassion, but Sasha's desire to have a caring mother figure didn't take into account her MIL's type (a Blamer) or her own DIL style (a Manager), nor the fact that her MIL believed her son could do no wrong. Instead of offering warmth or support, her MIL launched into deep criticisms of Sasha, telling her that she was acting inappropriately.

If you've found yourself moving silently through your home for days on end or known periods where it seems like one fight cycles into the next, I want you to know that you're not alone. One of the biggest breakthroughs I consistently have with clients comes when I get them to shift from focusing on *what* they're talking about (the kids, the in-laws, the mental load) to instead focusing on *how* they're talking about it. From my perspective, this entire event could have been avoided if Sasha and Nikhil knew how to practice healthy ways of communicating.

In this chapter, we're going to focus on shifting out of a "you versus me" mentality and building a sense of "we"-ness in its place. To do this, I'm going to walk you through three essential parts of communication and relationship dynamics: how to practice differentiation, how to break the cycle of repetitive fights, and how to avoid the communication errors that prevent sharing. Then I'll leave you with my top ten tips for healthy communication. By the end of the chapter, you'll be more prepared to start tackling conversations about your MIL and creating the relationship that works for you and your husband.

PRACTICING DIFFERENTIATION

A powerful principle to embody in your partnership is the idea that you are two separate people. It may sound obvious, but often we end up unconsciously believing two partners should view the world the same way, approach situations the same way, and even think and feel the same way. When we don't experience this "sameness," it can feel like a threat to a safe, loving, and committed relationship.

But remember, you didn't always feel this need to be exactly the same. Recall the early days of your relationship, when you and your partner first met. You had your own lives and interests, and there were parts of this person that excited and interested you precisely because they were foreign. You became attracted to who your partner was in the first place through their values and ways of approaching the world. But slowly, as partners' lives merge, they can end up growing emotionally fused.

I talked about emotional fusion in chapter 1 in the context of your husband and his mother; in an unhealthy mother-son relationship, the son might be expected to mirror all his mother's emotions, opinions, and habits instead of having his own separate inner life. But emotional fusion can also happen in a romantic relationship—and it's more common than you think. If one partner is upset about something and the other is not, the first partner may experience it as a betrayal. If one partner asks for time alone, the other may take it as a personal attack. Eventually, partners stop sharing their own feelings or opinions because they don't want to upset the other person, feel responsible for the other person's feelings, or feel guilty for having their own identities. Far from fostering closeness, this self-abandonment works against building healthy intimacy, as partners begin to feel resentment toward each other, fueling disconnection.

Sasha and Nikhil struggled to take in each other's perspectives. Nikhil perceived each comment or remark about his mother as a personal attack on him. He couldn't see that Sasha was having a separate experience and that this experience was not a judgment on whether he or his mother were good people.

The solution is to move away from codependency without running to the other extreme, hyperindependence. Today, our society thrives on messages like "Heal yourself," "The only person you can rely on is you," and "I'm not responsible for your feelings." However, this hyperindependent approach fails to take into account that we are biologically hardwired to need people, to need connection, and to give and receive care.

This is why a healthy relationship requires partners to practice *interdependence*, which brings autonomy and intimacy into balance. Autonomy is the ability to nurture and respect your own thoughts, feelings, desires, wishes, values, and needs. Intimacy is the interconnectedness that two people experience, a sense of feeling close to and known by each other. Interdependence prioritizes the "we" while respecting the autonomy of both individuals. One of the key skills in building this sense of "we are two separate people coming together" is the process of differentiation.

Differentiation is the ongoing ability to identify, make sense of, and share your internal experiences while also remaining connected to your partner by tolerating and accepting their ability to do the same. Differentiation is about using self-awareness and self-reflection to respond to the challenges in your relationship. Many of our day-to-day fights in a relationship are about a lack of differentiation: the inability to see that the other person has a different perspective and reflect on how we're being impacted by it.

There are four key skills to help you practice differentiation: self-awareness, self-regulation, acceptance of individual differences, and strong communication skills. Let's take a closer look at each one.

SELF-AWARENESS

Self-awareness is the ability to acknowledge your internal experiences, including your thoughts and feelings. The goal is not to react to them without thinking but rather to reflect and be curious about what is happening.

Try recognizing the thought patterns that frequently show up for you in your relationship. These thought patterns will include self-critical thoughts (e.g., "You never get it right," "You don't really matter to people") and negative thoughts about your partner (e.g., "He never helps out," "She always tells me what to do"). Start bringing awareness to hard moments with your partner. For example, if your husband is in a bad mood, start to see the impact it has on you instead of immediately reacting with your own bad mood.

Helpful statements to bring awareness to your current experience:

* "I notice . . ."

* "I'm having the thought that . . ."

* "When I see my husband do XYZ, I start to . . ."

SELF-REGULATION

There are always two choices when we experience a stimulus: React to it immediately in a knee-jerk manner, or respond with intentionality. Responding is often thought of as tapping into the "conscious mind" and requires you to slow down and self-regulate. For example, *reacting* to your husband's justification of his mother's behavior might mean that you snap back angrily and say, "This is just like last time." *Responding* would be saying something like "I'm having intense emotions about this, and I need a moment."

The following are skills you can use to help you self-regulate:

* Use grounding strategies. Push your feet into the floor. Take six slow breaths, counting in for four and out for six. Turn your neck slowly from side to side.

* Find a mantra that will help you slow down, such as "I don't have to respond immediately" or "We are both okay."

* Practice depersonalization by reminding yourself that statements or events are not reflections of your lovability or importance. Many of my clients like to repeat, "This isn't about me. They are allowed to have their feelings."

ACCEPTANCE OF INDIVIDUAL DIFFERENCES

You and your partner are two different people, and there will always be some differences between you. The goal is to accept these differences instead of trying to force each other to change. We want to shift from "How can I make you see it the same way I do?" to "How can we coexist together, knowing that we each have different ideas?"

It's important to remember that acceptance is different from liking. You might not *like* an opinion or habit of your partner's, but assuming it's not something that's actually abusive or harmful, you can accept that it is what it is. Acknowledging that we cannot control other people (and, likewise, they can't control us) will help us build more acceptance for our partners when differences arise.

STRONG COMMUNICATION SKILLS

Strong communication skills are essential for you and your partner to be a connected team—and absolutely necessary to solve your challenges related to your MIL. I'll leave you with ten tips at the end of this chapter, but here, I want to highlight two essential pieces every conversation needs.

The first is to be a good listener. We tend to listen to reply, instead of listening to really understand what the other person is saying. Curiosity is a way of being. Practice listening and asking questions to fully understand what is being shared.

The second is to offer empathy instead of solutions. It's essential to build compassion within our relationships instead of treating conversations like problems to solve—or, worse, opportunities to argue. Empathy and validation are more powerful tools that will leave the other person feeling understood.

Starting from this foundation will help you navigate any difficult conversations, including those about family dynamics and your MIL.

THE NEGATIVE INFINITY LOOP

Have you ever noticed that no matter *what* you're fighting about with your partner, the *way* you're fighting doesn't change? You might be having varying arguments about the dishes, your in-laws, or parenting, but the pattern of communication is the same each time. When I talk about these cycles, many people end up spiraling into self-blame, pointing fingers at their partner, or doubting whether they can change, so I want to emphasize this: You *can* interrupt and change the cycle by breaking the pattern. Even the most "successful" couples fall into these cycles sometimes, and neither one of you is to blame individually. What's important is to recognize that this pattern of communicating stops you from being able to feel close, share your vulnerabilities and fears, and, most important, solve your problems.

To help you understand your own communication cycles, I'm going to teach you about a concept from the emotionally focused couples therapy framework called the negative infinity loop.[1] We can break this loop down into what I call the "upstairs stuff" (surface-level reactions, assumptions, perceptions, and reactive emotions) and the "downstairs stuff" (deeper emotions, needs, and longings that sit at the core of who we are).

For example, Sasha frequently came to our sessions roiling with anger at Nikhil and his mother. This was her surface-level reaction—her upstairs stuff. For Nikhil, this anger brought up deep-rooted emotions and needs, like his fear of being inadequate. But because that was subconscious downstairs stuff, it wasn't immediately obvious to him. Instead, he focused on the upstairs experience that was easier to identify: He felt attacked.

In response to feeling criticized, Nikhil would grow defensive, dismissing what Sasha was saying and defending his mother, until eventually he'd tell Sasha that he no longer wanted to discuss the problem. But these upstairs reactions from Nikhil then affected Sasha's core emotions and needs, like the deep pain of feeling abandoned by her husband. But much like Nikhil, Sasha couldn't immediately recognize her downstairs stuff. Instead, it manifested on the upstairs level as vitriol. Sasha would express even more anger in an attempt to be heard and seen. And around they went in their cycle.

You   **Your Partner**

The "Upstairs Stuff"

Triggers and Reactions   Triggers and Reactions

Perceptions and Assumptions   Perceptions and Assumptions

Secondary/Reactive Emotions   Secondary/Reactive Emotions

Primary/Core Emotions   Primary/Core Emotions

Core Needs and Longings   Core Needs and Longings

The "Downstairs Stuff"

The goal of this framework is to shift your focus from whatever your current fight seems to be about on the surface to what is going on below the surface—what isn't being communicated but needs to be heard—so that you can start addressing what your problems are really about. Anytime you get stuck in a repeating fight, you and your partner can complete the exercise at the end of this section to figure out what started it and what is underneath it. Let's take a look at the negative infinity loop in more detail.

THE UPSTAIRS STUFF

In the context of the negative infinity loop, the upstairs stuff is the emotions, reactions, and stories we tell ourselves that happen closer to the surface. These are the thoughts and feelings that we find easier to consciously recognize and communicate. They're often repetitive in nature and, in the context of feeling disconnected in your relationship, are negative. I divide them into triggers and reactions, assumptions and perceptions, and secondary/reactive emotions.

Triggers and Reactions

The first component of the loop that keeps us stuck in negative communication cycles is triggers. Although people may use this word in casual conversation to mean a lot of things, in psychology, the word *trigger* has a specific meaning: an internal or external stimulus that leads to a negative physiological, cognitive, or emotional response. If you told your MIL not to come to the hospital until after you'd given birth but she showed up anyway, this might trigger a tight stomach, clenched jaw, and anger for you. Triggers often stem from early childhood experiences and past relationships. If your parents couldn't reliably afford gas when you were growing up, it might trigger anxiety for you when your partner leaves the gas tank empty without telling you.

Triggers are windows into what is happening deeper inside us, but they can also lead us to be reactive—to act without pausing, discerning, or fully understanding what's happening. If we stay at this reactive level, we will not do the deeper work, nor will we feel closer to or understood by our partners. Our job is to look at the downstairs stuff and make sense of it so that it doesn't keep surfacing in unhelpful ways. This is what understanding our triggers is about.

Clinical professor of psychiatry Dr. Dan Siegel writes that when we are triggered, our brains go "offline," which he refers to as "flip[ping] our lids."[2] In this moment, your actions are being guided by the parts of your brain that react to danger and threats. We want to be able to remain "online," with our actions guided by the parts of the brain responsible for executive functioning and rational thought. So while an empty gas tank might initially trigger fear and anxiety for you, you can pause and remind yourself that your husband works late, which is why he sometimes forgets to gas up the car.

Identifying the signs that indicate you're feeling triggered can help you bring awareness in these moments when you go offline. Sometimes acknowledging that something is pressing one of your buttons is enough to bring your rational brain back online. Here are some common physiological, emotional, and cognitive signs that you are triggered. In a journal or notebook, write down the ones you notice in yourself, and consider which ones your partner might also experience.

Talking fast	Sweating	Feeling disengaged
Raised voice	Fidgeting	Rapid blinking
Pounding heart	Irritability	Shaking leg
Feeling confused	Feeling overwhelmed	Crossed arms
Unable to think straight	Repeating the same thing	Blank face
Shortness of breath	Feeling like you're talking in circles	Feeling anxious
Feeling tired		

Learning to respond to your triggers is a key part of managing conflict with both your husband and your MIL (and anyone else, for that matter). Here are three powerful ways to respond to your triggers:

1. **Name it to tame it.** Say out loud what you're feeling: "I am so angry that this is happening right now" or "I'm feeling anxious about this visit." Naming your emotion or thought out loud is like lifting the lid on a pot; it prevents the water from boiling over.

2. **Give yourself a temperature shock.** When you're feeling overwhelmed, you can excuse yourself to splash cold water on your face, squeeze an ice cube, or place a frozen item on the back of your neck. This pulls your nervous system's attention away from the big emotion you're experiencing in the distressing moment.

3. **Step away from screens.** While many people choose to scroll on their phones to distract themselves from unpleasant feelings, staying stuck on screens can lead to further dysregulation of your nervous system. Instead, put on some music, move your body in the space that you're in, or go for a walk.

Assumptions and Perceptions

Once you've been able to identify your triggers, the next step in breaking negative communication cycles is to notice the types of assumptions and perceptions you're having about yourself and/or your partner. Sasha would notice Nikhil's body language change as soon as she brought up her struggles. He furrowed his eyebrows and crossed his arms. She would start to think, "He doesn't care about me," and make the assumption that he only cared about himself and his mother. For Nikhil, the trigger was his wife's tone of voice, which became higher and filled with deep sighs of frustration. In these moments, Nikhil immediately thought, "She's always coming at me. When will it ever be enough for her?" He made the assumption that Sasha thought his mother was a bad person and reacted defensively to it. Sasha and Nikhil struggled to see how their assumptions and perceptions were keeping them stuck.

Some common thoughts and assumptions that come up in my therapy room sound like:

* He should just know what my needs are.

* She's always asking me to do more. She's choosing to ignore all the things I do.

* They should put me first.

* There's no point in making an effort.

* They're overreacting.

* I have to deal with things all on my own.

* She's trying to hurt me.

* I'm not a priority.

We all see the world through our own lens, with our own biases and assumptions, but the fact is that you can't ever truly *know* what someone is thinking or what their motives are, which is why assumptions and perceptions get partners stuck in unhelpful cycles. They lead us to misinterpret our partner's words, actions, and body language, but more than that, they close us off from curiosity. The loss of curiosity has the biggest impact on the relationship, because it stops partners from being able to ask more questions before conflict escalates.

Here are some helpful questions to ask yourself to determine if you are getting stuck in your assumptions and perceptions:

* Is this a thought/feeling, or is it a fact?

* Are there parts of this experience that I don't completely understand yet?

* What else could be happening for my partner?

* How does thinking this help me with my partner?

* What is this assumption stopping me from really feeling?

Secondary/Reactive Emotions

Secondary emotions, also known as reactive emotions, are "reactions to reactions."[3] These more easily accessible emotions are typically unconscious attempts to protect you from deeper, more painful primary emotions (which we'll discuss next). These are reactions to the events—the things your partner said or did (or didn't say or do), the details of the situation, or even your assumptions about the situation.[4]

Common reactive emotions include the following:

Frustration	Anxiety	Confusion
Anger	Desperation	Contempt
Resentment	Overwhelm	Numbness
Detachment	Disappointment	Helplessness
Hopelessness	Depression	Jealousy
Guilt	Shame	

If you find yourself getting stuck in frustration and anger, I want to emphasize how much this makes sense given what you may have experienced in the past or in your current relationship. Many people don't learn how to talk about their primary emotions growing up, and many have parents who weren't able to respond to their emotions in helpful ways when they were young. Social conditioning can also be a contributing factor. For example, in therapy, many men stay stuck in feelings of irritation because they're taught early on to not express sadness or pain. Getting stuck at secondary emotions can create more conflict in relationships because it stops both you and the other person from understanding what you're truly feeling and what you really need.

THE DOWNSTAIRS STUFF

While the upstairs part of the negative infinity loop consists of more surface-level thoughts and feelings, the downstairs part consists of our deepest emotions and needs. Downstairs stuff is so deep that we're often not even conscious of it, but that doesn't make it any less real. I divide downstairs stuff into primary/core emotions and core needs and longings.

Primary/Core Emotions

Primary emotions, also known as core emotions, are deeper and harder to access than secondary emotions. They include sadness, pain, grief, and fear, and they often remain unconscious because consciously identifying them requires so much vulnerability. They're important to address, however, as they offer powerful ways of understanding what we need and how to move forward. They bring our partners closer to us and build a deeper understanding of ourselves.

Once you've identified your *secondary* emotion, ask yourself, "What is underneath this?" Sometimes the answer comes immediately, while other times it might take longer to uncover. To identify your primary core emotion, practice sitting in quiet and listening to yourself—not your thoughts but your feelings. You might ask yourself where else you have felt this before or where you feel this in your body.

Underneath Sasha's anger, she felt sad and hurt. With further exploration, she was able to identify that she feared she didn't matter to her husband. With the help of our work together, Nikhil shifted out of his defensive frustration and shared feeling small and inadequate with his wife when they got into their cycle; in his own way, he also feared that he didn't matter to her. This shift from their secondary emotions to the more vulnerable primary emotions helped each of them hear their partner's true experience and move into understanding what they actually needed to move forward.

Core Needs and Longings

Couples tend to get stuck in seeking the solution to their surface-level problem, but below the surface, each partner has core needs and longings that are not being fulfilled. There are eight core relational needs we all share. These are needs that everyone has, but different people might need them to be met in different ways and to different degrees—one person may have a higher need for safety, for example, while another may have a higher need for autonomy. Only when partners start trusting each other to meet each other's needs do they feel safe enough to start being able to problem-solve.

These core needs are as follows:

1. **Safety:** Safety is the state of feeling physically, emotionally, and psychologically secure in a relationship. This core need includes the ability to express your thoughts, feelings, and desires without being attacked or punished. It's about being able to be authentic and vulnerable, knowing that your partner will not use your vulnerability as a weapon. You can openly share your insecurities, trusting that the other person will respond in an accepting manner. When this need is being met,

you don't fear judgment, abandonment, or rejection. When it's not being met, you might feel anxious, uncertain, or guarded in your relationship.

2. **Love and Belonging:** To feel a sense of love and belonging is to know that your partner cares for you and that they're acting with your best interest in mind. It's knowing that the answer to questions like "Do I belong here?," "Do I matter?," and "Am I loved?" is yes. At the core of secure relationships, we want to know that we're in this together. Engaging in acts of belonging also means sharing important updates and information and being transparent about motives and intentions. This includes sharing hard things and working through upset feelings together.

3. **Attention:** We often connect the core need for attention to being "needy" because of the messaging we receive as kids that you shouldn't be an "attention seeker." Yet everyone has the need to feel seen, heard, and valued in their partnership. This core need asks the question, "When I need you, will you pay attention to me?" Giving attention is not just being physically present; it's about actively listening, giving undivided focus, and showing interest in your partner's thoughts, feelings, and experiences. When attention is given, it builds emotional intimacy, letting the other person know that you see them for who they are.

4. **Validation and Recognition:** Validation is the act of acknowledging and accepting your partner's feelings without judging them. The core need for validation is to ask your partner to listen with empathy and to understand your experience. Giving someone validation does not necessarily mean you agree with them, but

it does mean you're helping them to feel heard,
seen, and understood. This goes hand in hand with
recognition, which is the need to be seen for who
you are, what you bring to the relationship, and your
contributions to all areas of the relationship and
your shared life together.

5. **Connection and Intimacy:** Connection and intimacy are
all about time together, affection, and physical and
emotional closeness. I use the word *intimacy* carefully
here, because people tend to narrowly define it as having
to do with sex. In reality, there are many different types
of intimacy: emotional, physical, sexual, spiritual or
value-based, experiential, and intellectual. A relationship
needs some sense of intimacy and connection, including
physical touch like hugging, kissing, and holding hands.
An important note is that sex is not a core need in and
of itself and shouldn't be requested or demanded on
those terms. Sex can be an important part of intimacy,
but there are many other ways to explore the core need
for connection and feeling close to someone.

6. **Power and Agency:** We tend to view power as power
"over" someone else, but that's not actually what this
core need is about. Power as a core need is about having
a sense of agency and influence in a relationship. It's
important to feel that your wishes, choices, and desires
actually matter. Many people end up unintentionally
giving up their power, which leads to them not getting
their needs met and also to more codependent
relationships. When our need for agency isn't being
met, we implicitly say, "Your wishes and choices are
more important than mine." When this need is being met,
we build confidence in the knowledge that each partner
respects the other's choices, which is ultimately part

of the "we" that is needed for differentiation and a healthy partnership.

7. **Freedom and Autonomy:** While the core need for power and agency is concerned with feeling that your choices and opinions matter to your partner, the need for freedom and autonomy is about independence and exploration. This is the desire to nurture your own individuality and connect to your own interests outside the relationship, trusting that you will be welcomed back to share those experiences within your partnership. When partners cultivate their separate friends and personal hobbies, it offers them a chance to come back together with a renewed sense of curiosity and desire to connect. Those with a lower need for autonomy might "do everything together," and this might work fine for them. However, many couples who struggle with desire for each other ultimately find that it stems from having lost their sense of freedom. I encourage all couples to find ways to nurture their individuality.

8. **Play and Fun:** After the "honeymoon stage," which lasts between six months and a year, couples often lose a sense of play and fun in their relationship—but it remains a core need. Play is all about exploration, curiosity, humor, and spontaneity. We all need play and fun in some way, and when we engage in activities that spark joy and laughter, we experience more bonding moments and overall intimacy together. This is not about just finding another restaurant to try for date night. Yes, play and fun can be about the types of activities you do together, but they are also about finding the laughter and whimsy in everyday moments. Meeting this core need helps to balance the stress that comes

with the challenges in life, especially as you navigate a tricky relationship with your MIL.

In addition to those fundamental needs, we all have our own deep longings. In my clinical experience, I've noticed that many of these core longings stem from childhood wounds. A child who grew up in a home where they were never listened to longs for respect. A child who was never recognized for who they are or how well they were doing longs for validation. Here is a list of common longings and fears in our relationships.

LONGINGS	FEARS
To be accepted for who I am	Being abandoned
To be validated	Being inadequate or unworthy
To feel closer to my partner	Not measuring up
To feel important/ like I matter	Being a failure
To feel safe	Not being accepted or valued
To be held	Being rejected
To be acknowledged	Being unlovable
To be respected	Being controlled

In considering core longings and needs, Sasha was able to connect her need for respect to never feeling listened to as a child, and Nikhil was able to ask for specific examples of how he could show her the respect she needed. Nikhil's need for reassurance stemmed from his mother never recognizing his accomplishments, even today while living under his roof. Sasha acknowledged that she could be better at expressing her appreciation and gratitude for the things he did do.

Exercise:

Completing Your Negative Infinity Loop

Now that you can see the steps contributing to your negative cycles, it's time to change how you communicate with your partner, using this simple exercise. Think back to your last argument. How did it start? What was said or done? With this argument in mind, answer the following questions (which will complete your side of the infinity loop). If your partner is willing, have him answer the questions (which will complete his side of the infinity loop). If he's not willing to do the exercise with you, you can likely guess what many of his responses would be, but be careful about your assumptions; it's especially important to be curious about his primary/core emotions and his core needs and longings.

A key piece of this exercise is to practice being able to tell your partner about your primary core emotion and need instead of focusing on their behaviors, your/their reactive emotions, and/or the assumptions you're making. When you focus on information above the line (the upstairs stuff), you're more likely to get stuck in your cycle.

First, answer these questions about the upstairs stuff:

* **Triggers and Reactions:** When I got triggered, what did I do (e.g., blame, poke, defend, guard myself)?

* **Perceptions and Assumptions:** What did I perceive from my partner? What assumptions did I make about my partner and myself? What story am I telling myself?

* **Secondary/Reactive Emotions:** As I told myself this story, what did I feel?

Next, answer these questions about the downstairs stuff:

* **Primary/Core Emotions:** Deep down, what did I feel?

* **Core Needs and Longings:** Complete the following sentences: When I feel this, I need [need]. And what would be helpful is [specific and clear action].

Once you have completed these questions, you can identify your negative infinity loop by completing this sentence:

The more you [insert partner's reaction], the more I [insert your reaction]. The story I tell myself is [insert your perception/ assumption]. But underneath this, what you don't see is that I feel [insert your primary/core emotion] and need [insert your core need and longing].

PREVENTING COMMUNICATION CATASTROPHES

Now that you've learned how to practice differentiation and break the cycle of repetitive fights, let's dig into a few communication errors you might be making and how to stop making them. After researching thousands of couples, psychologists Drs. John and Julie Gottman identified four dysfunctional ways of communicating that predicted divorce: criticism, defensiveness, contempt, and stonewalling. They named them "the four horsemen of the apocalypse" given just how catastrophic they were when used long-term.[5] While this section focuses on how these modes of communication affect couples, as you read, I encourage you to think of how they might also show up between you and your MIL or between your MIL and your husband.

CRITICISM

Criticism blames and attacks the character of the other person. It's a deflection tool that places ownership and responsibility on others in order to protect yourself from feeling uncomfortable.

This style of communication triggers defensiveness from others and prevents them from being able to understand what is happening to you.

Examples of criticism include:

*   "You always let your mother interfere."

*   "You never clean up after yourself."

*   "You're always prioritizing your family over mine."

*   "You never listen to me. You only think of yourself."

How can you communicate without resorting to criticism? Here are a few strategies:

*   State the emotion you're feeling and connect it to what you need. For example: "I feel like an outsider when you make plans with your family without me. This hurts, and I need you to include me."

*   Ask for what you need using a positive reframe. Instead of saying, "You don't help out around the house," be specific and say, "I need your help with the dishes tonight."

*   Share vulnerable feelings like sadness, fear, and grief.

*   Practice expressing complaints that focus on the challenge at hand, not on blaming the other person. Instead of "You never listen to my needs about family visits," try "Having your whole family here is a lot to figure out."

*   Express less. If you lean into blame, it's likely because you've spent a lifetime not being heard or listened to. You learned that the only way to be seen is to up the ante.

Practice using fewer words and trusting that your point will still be made.

DEFENSIVENESS

Defensiveness is minimizing or refuting what the other person is saying as a way to refuse to take responsibility. There are three D's we can look out for when it comes to defensiveness.

* **Deflection:** Taking your concern and placing it on another person or back on you. ("Well, if you weren't so anxious, this wouldn't be an issue with my mom.")

* **Dismissal:** Minimizing the other person's feelings or the impact of what happened. ("It's not really a big deal. You're blowing this out of proportion.")

* **Denial:** Refusing to acknowledge that anything happened. ("I don't think there's anything to address here.")

Note that defensiveness is *not* the same thing as gaslighting, which is the *intentional* act of leading someone to self-doubt and lowered self-esteem. Defensiveness stems from a lack of awareness of communication patterns. Many of my clients are surprised to learn that they're even responding in a defensive manner, indicating that it's not their intent to make the other person feel small or dismissed.

Strategies to communicate without defensiveness include:

* Slow down your responses. Try cultivating the habit of responding with "Thank you for sharing this with me" or "Tell me more about that."

* Ask questions. Be curious. Remind yourself that you're on the same team and work to gather more information.

* Practice taking accountability for how your actions impact your partner. This doesn't mean they're right and you're wrong; it means you're willing to prioritize the relationship and address how you hurt your partner.

* Take a break and return to the conversation later if you feel unable to respond without being defensive. Set a time to come back to it so the issue doesn't get forgotten.

CONTEMPT

Contempt is a low opinion of or lack of regard for another person. If you have contempt for someone, you start seeing only negative qualities in them and believing them to be inferior or bad. People often express contempt through hostile humor and denigrating comments meant to put the other person down, such as "Well, I wouldn't expect you to stand up for me because you can never say no to your mom" or "It's okay, I'll do it myself because I know you'll just screw it up." An insidious strategy, this communication breaks down security and connection.

Strategies for changing contemptuous communication include:

* Cultivate compassion toward your partner. View them with the same kindness that you would want them to view you.

* Prioritize respect. Strong communication requires respecting both you and your partner.

STONEWALLING AND WITHDRAWING

Stonewalling is a refusal to engage with your partner at all, as if you were building an impassable barrier between the two of you.

When hard conversations arose, Nikhil repeatedly walked away from Sasha. He was doing this to try to protect himself from getting hurt, but his withdrawal left Sasha feeling he didn't care about her or the issue. Research by developmental psychologist Dr. Ed Tronick shows that when caregivers shut down, toddlers enter into primal panic and distress, demonstrating what happens when our attachment figures are no longer accessible and responsive.[6] A version of this primal panic and distress can occur even for adults, which is why stonewalling leads to deep feelings of insecurity and rejection.

Here are some strategies to use instead of stonewalling and withdrawal:

* Practice self-soothing techniques such as deep breathing, progressive muscular relaxation (squeezing different body parts for five seconds and then releasing), or grounding (pushing your feet into the floor).

* Vocalize when you're feeling overwhelmed so your partner can understand you're not simply refusing to participate in the conversation.

* Agree on a cue word you can use to indicate you need a time-out.

* Schedule specific times for conversations. Regular check-ins foster the norm in your relationship that you can talk about important issues, positive or negative. The more you practice, the easier these conversations become.

* Engage in a physical activity while having hard conversations, such as walking or doing dishes side by side.

TEN RULES FOR HEALTHY COMMUNICATION

When you have adaptive, constructive ways to manage conflict and communicate what you're feeling and needing, there is an opportunity for deeper relational development. Here are the top ten rules for communication that I give all my clients. They'll help you get out of the "you versus me" mindset and develop a sense of "we"—not just in your marriage but also in your dynamic with your MIL.

ASSUME POSITIVE INTENTIONS

Go into conversations with your partner with the view that they have positive intentions. This perspective shift goes a long way in a partnership. By removing the assumption of malicious intent, you're giving them the benefit of the doubt and the opportunity to repair mistakes. Our brains are designed to scan for threat, so naturally we tend to look for the negatives in what someone is saying and doing (or not saying and doing). This means it might take intentional effort to see the good in your partner, but remind yourself that your partner has chosen you and wants to work through this with you. Most partners want to resolve conflict and get back to feeling good again, even if they don't know how to do this just yet.

BE ON THE SAME TEAM

Couples frequently get stuck playing a metaphorical game of singles tennis. They're on opposite sides of the net, with a narrow focus on the issue "coming at" them (such as a mother-in-law's behavior). Instead of seeking match point, focus on playing doubles. View the problem coming across the net as something you choose to tackle together. A statement like "We're on the same team" can be a powerful reminder in hard moments. This invites us to step out of a "you versus me" (or "you and your mother versus me") POV and into the "we" perspective that is so important for connection.

SPEAK WITH KINDNESS

Before saying something, ask yourself how you would phrase this to your dearest friend. Then ask yourself, "How would I want to hear this information?" In our intimate relationships, we hopefully build a sense of security knowing that our partner is always there with us. Unfortunately, with time and deepening of the bond, couples can start to take each other for granted and grow more irritable with each other. It's important to keep delivering words with kindness and compassion. During challenging times, this might sound like "This is hard" or "I see you trying to navigate this."

STICK TO ONE ISSUE

When trying to solve conflict, partners often bring up past hurts as a way to validate the hurt they feel in the moment. In a conversation about establishing boundaries on your holiday schedule, you might feel tempted to list all the hurts that your MIL has ever caused you. I call this "lawyering up" or "piling on," and it doesn't help couples solve the current issue.

A powerful strategy for you to practice when communicating your feelings is to first remind yourself that you do not need to justify your experience. Your feelings are real. From here, the conversation will be more productive if you focus on this event and your feelings now. If you find old events continuing to show up in conversation, a helpful strategy is writing a letter listing all those hurts, then throwing it away or ripping it up. Processing our emotions by handwriting is a great exercise that allows the brain to release the wounds.

USE A SOFT START-UP

Start a difficult conversation by talking about what is going well in your relationship. We tend to point out the negative, leaving the other person feeling unappreciated and unseen for how they show up in the relationship. Ask if your partner has time to talk and begin by sharing something that you're grateful for about your partner and relationship.

Soft start-ups use "I" language. Anytime you start a sentence with "You . . ." or "Your mother . . . ," you trigger defensiveness from your partner. When you express yourself by starting your sentences with "I," you're being more vulnerable and helping the other person understand your core emotions. You're also giving yourself a sense of agency and power, even when you can't control how your partner is going to respond.

VALIDATE EACH OTHER

When partners validate what the other person is saying, it brings them closer together and deepens understanding. This might sound like "I see that you're sad we haven't had time to talk about this," "I hear that you're upset that my mother didn't acknowledge you," or "I understand you wish things were different." Validation communicates clearly to your partner that you're paying attention to them, you understand them, and you hold empathy and a nonjudgmental position. It says that you see the facts or the truth of *their* perspective, even if you hold a different one.

Validation doesn't necessarily mean that you agree with your husband or think he's right, or vice versa. It simply means that you both see and accept each other's emotions or experience. I like to use the analogy of a bridge. You and your partner stand on opposite sides of the bridge, each having a different viewpoint. To truly validate and understand your partner's internal world, you need to cross the bridge to see what they're looking at and experience it from their perspective. Taking turns crossing the bridge is what creates bidirectional validation.

AGREE TO DISAGREE

The desire to have your partner agree with you stems from a vulnerable belief that if others agree with you, it means that you are valid, worthy, and enough. This is particularly true for people who are more anxious in their relationships. But the truth is that "sameness"—agreeing on all issues and viewing things in the same way—only provides a false sense of security. Healthy relationships are founded in recognizing that you are two separate people. The goal is not to get the other person to agree with you but instead to create greater understanding and compassion between two people. Remember: You are neither right nor wrong. You are both okay.

TAKE BREAKS

When you feel your conversation getting stuck in your negative infinity loop, it's imperative that you stop the cycle and take a break. It doesn't matter who stops the conversation, but one person needs to be able to press pause. When you're in the depths of these cycles, you don't feel emotionally safe, which makes it impossible to solve a problem, so taking a break is not giving up—it's actually more productive than trying to push through.

Some couples find it helpful to choose a "safe" word or a metaphor to indicate they are getting stuck in the cycle (e.g., "I think we're spinning in the washing machine again"). Research shows that a break needs to be twenty to thirty minutes long to help your nervous system come back to a calm and regulated state.[7] During the break, engage in a task that helps you to feel grounded and calmer. Be sure to make a plan for when you'll come back to the conversation so that neither partner is left hanging.

AVOID TAKING IT PERSONALLY

During a tense discussion, it's easy to feel that any statement is a personal attack on you. That's why one of the best things you can do in hard conversations is to remind yourself that your partner is also having a difficult time and your job is to get curious about their experience. While it may feel deeply personal, it isn't only about you.

If your partner is using "you" language ("You're doing X," "You always say Y"), invite them to try restating what they've just said using "I" language or to share more about what they're feeling on the inside. Hold in mind that what they're saying is not a statement about your worthiness or lovability.

ASK IF THEY WANT YOU TO PROBLEM SOLVE OR JUST LISTEN

We can all think of that person in our life who's ready to offer a solution any time we have a problem but who doesn't always leave us feeling heard and understood. When people jump into problem-solving, it's often to try to relieve their own internal sense of discomfort at what is being expressed. Of course they want to help their loved one as well, but offering solutions before someone asks for them can leave that person feeling unseen and unheard, triggering negative communication cycles.

If your instinct is to dive straight into problem-solving, practice asking your partner how you can support them after they share something. If what they want is validation, to hear your feelings, or just someone to listen, offer them that. If your partner tends to be the expert problem solver, remind yourself that they have positive intentions and gently redirect them to meeting the need you have in that moment.

PUTTING IT IN THE VAULT

We've covered a lot of ground in part I of this book. We looked at the unique relationship between mother-in-law and daughter-in-law, the dynamics at play between your husband and his mother, the dynamics in your own family of origin that affect how you approach relationships today, and the communication strategies necessary to get on the same team as your partner. Now that we understand these fundamentals, it's time to roll up our sleeves and start problem-solving. In part II, I'll teach you how to implement the VAULT method: Values, Aspirations, Understanding Your Triangle, Limits and Boundaries, and Taking Action. The goal of the VAULT is to build a safe and secure relationship that is sound in structure against the outside forces that can impact your marital bond. I developed this five-step method over years of clinical practice, and I've seen it help many women establish healthy relationships with their mothers-in-law. I hope it will help you do the same.

PART II

The VAULT Method

Values, Aspirations, Understanding Your Triangle,
Limits and Boundaries, Taking Action

Chapter 5

VALUES

―――――

ou chose your partner, but you didn't choose his mother or the conflict that so often comes with this in-law dynamic. Like many of the women I've worked with, you might find yourself feeling there is no pathway forward. Maybe you appease, keep the peace, and try to play the good girl, stepping into a victim role, only to be met with toxic behavior and communication cycles. On the other hand, maybe you feel like the villain because trying to advocate for yourself and/or your children always seems to set you against your mother-in-law and your husband.

I believe that you don't need to feel like the victim or the villain. Instead, I want to invite you, the daughter-in-law, to become your own main character and take a seat at the table in a position that aligns with and prioritizes your marriage.

After working with thousands of women and couples, it became clear to me that there was an urgent need for a method to help people navigate their MIL challenges while also strengthening their relationships with their partners. I came up with the VAULT method to help couples have important conversations, be on the same team, and find the best approach to move forward. I chose the name "VAULT" because the approach lets you and your partner create a sound structure that helps keep the relational bond intact. What does VAULT stand for?

* **Values:** Determine what you find meaningful and worth prioritizing, in your life and in your relationship.

* **Aspirations:** Decide what you desire and expect in your relationship moving forward.

* **Understanding Your Triangle:** Closely examine the three-way dynamic between you, your husband, and his mother that got you here—so you can understand what to do to change it.

* **Limits and Boundaries:** Figure out what healthy boundaries look like for you and how to set them.

* **Taking Action:** Put what you've learned into practice and create the relationship you want with your MIL.

The goal of each step in the VAULT system is to provide you with new skills as a couple so that you can create healthy boundaries and renegotiate your connection with your MIL as a team. You can build the relationship that you want with your MIL, one that considers the needs and values of everyone involved. It will take work, but the work will pay off (and if your husband is having trouble with the work, direct him to Appendix B, which provides five tips to help him through). Ultimately, your marriage will be stronger for it.

Let's get started with the first step in the VAULT method: values.

THE IMPORTANCE OF VALUES

Every summer, Julie and Damion made a trip to his family's vacation house, and every summer, they spiraled into arguments about how to deal with his mother. Damion's mother would frequently play the victim card, true to her Victim MIL type. She'd spend the entire visit needling them with comments like "I wish you could have arrived Friday night, but I guess Julie had to work" and "If I had a man around the house, it would be less expensive to maintain, and I wouldn't have to rent it out for July."

This last comment was especially hurtful to Damion because it made him feel pressure to take the place of his father, who had abandoned the family when he was a child. Damion had spent his life trying to meet his mother's outsize needs, but he could never replace his father, and in trying, he'd never gotten to be the kid in the relationship. But when Julie expressed her frustration with how his mother was treating him, instead of feeling seen, Damion would turn on her, demanding that she have more patience and compassion for his mother. At this point, they would end up spiraling into their negative cycle.

Like many couples, Julie and Damion tried to solve the problem by focusing on the short-term goal they needed to accomplish—in this case, getting through the vacation. They thought if they could ignore Damion's mom's comments and keep the peace for just a little while longer, they could go back home and forget all this fighting. But they were making the fundamental mistake of failing to look at the bigger picture. As a result, they remained stuck in the same dilemma every year, which only created more and more dread and resentment in both of them.

This is why the first step of the VAULT method requires couples to step out of narrowly focusing on immediate outcomes and instead define their shared values and identify what is truly meaningful to them.

WHAT ARE VALUES?

In session, Damion looked confused when I asked him what his values were. I rephrased the question: "Tell me what's really important to you."

After a long pause, he said, "Well, my mom is important. I should be spending time with her, and it's my job to help her, to be a supportive son. My family is important to me, my wife. I really don't get enough time to see my grandparents, and they're getting older, so I should be going out to see them." From here, Damion started to tell me about how Julie is close to her family and sees them several times a month, and he felt guilty that he didn't have the same level of closeness with his mother.

At this point, I could tell Damion was no longer talking about his values and had shifted into talking about his desires and expectations. While desires and expectations are helpful in guiding us to take action, when we focus on them without being rooted in our values, we get stuck. Sometimes we set goals that are not in line with what matters to us but rather with what we think "should" matter to us. This can happen when we're comparing ourselves to others, basing our actions on guilt, or prioritizing someone else's happiness at the expense of our own. Far from getting you what you want, this is a surefire way to become disconnected from yourself and grow resentful.

This is what was happening for Damion. The point here is not that he "shouldn't" spend time with his mother or help her with household tasks. The point is that his desire to do this was largely coming from a place of guilt, insecurity, and a need to placate his mother's sense of victimhood, all of which led him to continue to feed the cycle between him and his mom.

As the first step in the VAULT method, I teach people to step out of these kinds of expectations and instead examine their values. Most people look at me with a quizzical expression when I ask them what their values are. They know they try to exercise regularly, use gentle parenting with their kids, check in on their aging parents, and volunteer. Rarely do they know what guides them in making these choices. When it comes to values, we can ask ourselves fundamental questions like:

* What is important to me?

* What *really* matters?

* What helps me to build a rich and fulfilling life?

* What kind of person do I want to be?

* If there were no barriers, what would I be focusing on in life?

* What do I stand for?

Values are a compass. They guide us through making daily decisions, helping us answer the question "Am I heading in the direction I want to be headed?" When we live aligned with what is important to us, we are more likely to experience a purposeful and rich life and less likely to experience dissatisfaction, restlessness, and depression.[1]

Your values are constructed by previous experiences, significant events, and your cultural upbringing. Values also change and grow as you evolve. For example, as a parent to an infant, you might value creating safety and routine, but as a parent to a teenager, your value might shift to creating autonomy and connection. Unless values are explicitly stated, we can only guess each other's by observing the actions we take: "I can see your relationship is important to you because every Friday night you commit to date night."

It might feel difficult to identify what you value, especially if you or your partner were raised in families in which you were expected to care for others' needs above your own. If that's the case, it can be helpful to reflect on where you put your energy each day. If you spend a lot of time talking to friends, for example, friendship is probably important to you. And if you reflect on your daily acts and you notice that you *don't* feel good about where your energy is going, take this as important information to start reprioritizing. If all that time with friends is leaving you exhausted and stretched too thin, maybe you find quiet intro-spective time more valuable than you realized.

Values are different from feelings. You might have feelings *about* your values, but when you start a sentence with "I feel" or "I feel like," you're likely talking about emotions or thoughts, not values.

Values are also different from goals. While values guide how we move forward, goals are about what we're moving toward. They focus on a desired outcome, whether that's getting a job or setting aside weekly time with your partner. Ideally, our values drive our goals. For example, if you have a value of financial se-curity or leadership, you might work toward the goal of getting a promotion at work.

Here are some examples of values and how they relate to goals.

VALUE	GOAL
Family	Have family dinner every Sunday night
My relationship	Schedule ten minutes to connect with my partner at the end of the day
My children	Put away my phone while playing with my kids
Connection	Share something vulnerable with someone
Personal growth	Read a self-help book

Exercise:

Your Fiftieth Wedding Anniversary

Imagine you reach your fiftieth wedding anniversary. It's a huge milestone! How do you decide to celebrate? A party? A trip with family? A small gathering? Picture who is at the event with you and what the room looks like. If your partner were to give a toast, what do you hope they would say about the last fifty years you've spent together? How do you wish they would describe you—the choices you made, the ways you showed up, your character? Now imagine they talk about a hard time in your relationship. How would they describe the way you walked through it? What do you wish they'd remember about that hard moment and the way you showed up? The answers to these questions will help you shed light on your values.

QUIETING THE OUTSIDE NOISE

We all receive messages from our culture, religion, family upbringing, and so on about what makes a "good" person or a "normal" family or what we "should" or "shouldn't" be focusing on. It can be hard to separate these messages from what we really value. Damion, for example, spent most of his life trying to please his mother and fill in for his absent father, first with basketball and schoolwork, and later by checking off the boxes of adulthood, like getting promoted, getting married, and buying a home. He struggled to know what his values were and instead made decisions based on the urge to please, to care for his mother, and above all, to avoid feeling guilty.

It can be especially hard to discern our values during seasons of life that demand a lot of resources, like a job change, a big move, or the birth of a baby. When we're just trying to make it through the night with a colicky newborn, it becomes hard to focus on anything else. But when we're busy looking outward at immediate problems—instead of inward for our true sense of knowing—we are more at risk of making choices that are not aligned with our values, which leads us down a path of not feeling connected with ourselves or our partner.

Here are some questions to help you focus inward:

* Am I comparing myself to someone else or to an external standard?

* How is my desire to be right or "good enough" contributing to the choice I'm making?

* Am I making this decision from a place of lacking or fear?

* Am I making this decision based on what I "should" or "must" do?

* How will I feel about this in two years? Five years?

* Am I saying yes in the service of keeping someone else happy?

* Am I giving up something that is important to me in order to avoid feeling guilty?

If you're struggling to find what is important to you, it might be time to quiet the outside noise. It can be a reflex to grab your phone or to wonder what others think about what you're doing, but you can practice repeatedly coming back to sitting with your own self. Spend ten minutes at the start of your day without looking at any kind of media or thinking about other people. This might feel uncomfortable for you, as it did for Damion when he had to start examining the autopilot behaviors that were leading him to feel further away from what was important to him. But the benefits are worth it.

GENERATIONAL DIFFERENCES IN VALUES

My clients often tell me stories of their parents discussing lifestyle choices as if they were moral laws. They want to instruct their adult children in the "right" financial decisions, parenting decisions, and even etiquette decisions. My clients struggle with a deep sense that in order to be worthy, they have to follow these "correct" guidelines, even if they don't agree with them. If your parents or in-laws think your house should always be organized and cleaned or insist you have to visit every Sunday night, you might be left feeling like you're failing or not good enough.

As KC Davis writes in her bestselling book, *How to Keep House While Drowning*, tasks like folding laundry, doing the dishes, and mopping the floor are "morally neutral."[2] It doesn't make you a bad person if you don't have neatly folded clothing or if the dishes aren't done. So how did we end up attaching so much moral value to them? If a dear friend did something your parents' generation has labeled "wrong," would you view them as being bad? If your child told you they engaged in this behavior, would you think they were unworthy? This philosophy of moral neutrality also extends to how you decide to engage in holidays, visits with family, or choosing what matters to you.

The couples I work with are trying to break away from this "right or wrong" paradigm and instead make decisions based on their own values rather than the previous generation's. They are saying things like "We only get two weeks off a year, and we want to see the world, so we can't spend them both visiting family." This isn't to disrespect what it means to have family and share intergenerational wisdom, experiences, and stories. It's to acknowledge that modern couples don't want to accept moral dogma they don't agree with based on a top-down family hierarchy. Younger generations are saying, "That doesn't work for us," and discovering a new sense of agency in our families.

In order to build a secure partnership and move forward as a connected couple, you will want to consider where your decisions come from: Are they coming from your parents' or in-laws' ideas about how "this is just what you do," or are they rooted in your values and what you and your family need?

Exercise:
Discovering Your Values

What do you really want? What are your desires for you as an individual and a couple? In this three-part exercise, you'll first look within yourself to determine your own values, then work with your partner to identify your values as a couple, and finally make plans to put those values into action. Note that you won't actually talk a lot about your MIL in this stage of the VAULT method, as values are something specific to you and your partner. You need to define this between the two of you before you can focus on the next step.

Part 1:
Your Guiding Values

In this part of the exercise, you'll identify what really matters to you. Each partner should complete this part separately, in their own journal or notebook.

1. On the list of one hundred values below, jot down the ten to fifteen values that mean the most to you.[3] These are the things you consider most important in your life. (If you chose fewer than ten, go through the list again and choose a few more. Sometimes you don't catch everything on the first pass.)

Abundance	Ambition	Benevolence	Charity
Acceptance	Appreciation	Boldness	Cheerfulness
Accountability	Attractiveness	Brilliance	Cleverness
Achievement	Autonomy	Calmness	Collaboration
Adventure	Balance	Caring	Community
Advocacy	Being the Best	Challenge	Commitment

Compassion

Consistency

Contribution

Cooperation

Creativity

Credibility

Curiosity

Daring

Decisiveness

Dedication

Dependability

Diversity

Empathy

Encouragement

Enthusiasm

Ethics

Excellence

Expressiveness

Fairness

Family

Flexibility

Friendships

Freedom

Fun

Generosity

Grace

Growth

Happiness

Health

Honesty

Humility

Humor

Inclusiveness

Independence

Individuality

Innovation

Inspiration

Intelligence

Intuition

Joy

Kindness

Knowledge

Leadership

Learning

Love

Loyalty

Making a
Difference

Mindfulness

Motivation

Optimism

Open-
Mindedness

Originality

Passion

Performance

Personal
Development

Peace

Perfection

Playfulness

Popularity

Power

Preparedness

Proactivity

Professionalism

Punctuality

Quality

Recognition

Relationships

Reliability

Resilience

Resourcefulness

Responsibility

Responsiveness

Risk Taking

Safety

Security

Self-Control

Selflessness

Service

Simplicity

Spirituality

Stability

Success

Teamwork

Thankfulness

Thoughtfulness

Traditionalism

Trustworthiness

Understanding

Uniqueness

Usefulness

Versatility

Vision

Warmth

Wealth

Well-Being

Wisdom

Zeal

2. Once you have ten to fifteen values identified, group them into three or four categories based on your own instincts. For example, you might put *leadership, guidance,* and *knowledge* in one group together. Your groupings are totally up to you; do whatever feels right.

3. Pick a title for each group of values. For example, if you have a group containing *acceptance, compassion,* and *love,* you might name the group "Kindness." If you have *dependability, family,* and *security* together, you might name the group "Connection."

4. Now write a list of the titles you chose. These are your Guiding Values.

5. Rank your Guiding Values in order from most important to least important. If you find yourself getting stuck, try writing a sentence to define that value in your life. Or complete this sentence: "If I could work on only one of these areas, it would be . . ."

6. Last, write answers to the following questions: Which of these values are the most important to me? Which ones am I living out or not living out? If I could choose one value to focus on today, what would it be?

Part 2: Your Shared Values

Now that you've both thought deeply about your personal values, it's time for you and your partner to discuss your shared values as a couple. Complete this part of the exercise together.

1. Take turns sharing your lists of Guiding Values with each other. You'll notice that you each hold different

values. This is okay—and to be expected! You are two autonomous individuals coming together in a relationship. The goal here is to build curiosity and understanding. You don't need to argue with the other person or defend your values. Instead, be open to what is being shared with you. There is no right, wrong, or "superior" value.

2. Take notice of any values that overlap. Rewrite these values together so you can each understand them and use them to make future goals. Given that we're working on relationships, be sure to discuss how values related to relationship and family show up for each of you.

3. Discuss the following questions with each other: What are the top two values we want to focus on right now? What support do you need to live out your values? Do we have any values that don't align, and if so, how can we make space for these differing values?

Part 3:
Living Aligned with Your Values

Now that you've explored your actions individually and as a couple, it's time to think about how to put them into action. Looking at your list of values as a couple, set some goals together for each value. Make the goals small and attainable. For example, if you're looking at the value of your relationship, a goal might be "Spend ten minutes together at the end of the day" or "Send each other lunchtime texts." These are small things you can do that keep you engaged with your value and help you feel like you're on the same team. Write a list of these goals and choose one to act on each day.

LIVING ALIGNED WITH YOUR VALUES

Once you've done the work to determine what your values are, you might not know exactly what to do with them. Let's explore some key areas to consider in helping you put your values into action in your life.

PSYCHOLOGICAL FLEXIBILITY

Psychological flexibility is about bringing awareness to your thoughts, feelings, and urges, and then, instead of being ruled by these internal experiences, discerning which actions align with what is truly meaningful to you.[4] Sometimes we can approach situations with a level of rigidity about our values that prevents us from collaborating with our partner. This might be particularly true if we've been hurt by our MIL, feel like an outsider, or feel exhausted by the family's dynamics. Remember that the goal of identifying your values is to create a collaborative space for you and your partner. If one of you digs in about having the "right" or "better" value, you're operating counter to the larger goal of greater understanding within your relationship.

DEALING WITH GUILT

Guilt is an emotion that tells you you've done something bad, and it can be a valuable signal that it's time to change course or make amends. However, I've noticed that guilt frequently shows up in two situations where you *haven't* done anything wrong: when you're choosing to do something that seems to conflict with one of your values (e.g., you feel guilty setting a boundary with your MIL because family connection is one of your top values), and when someone you care about is having difficult feelings (e.g., your MIL is upset by your boundary). When you avoid doing what matters to you, you end up in a vicious cycle: The more you avoid it, the more guilt you feel. It's helpful to name guilt and acknowledge it, but don't let it stop you from making important—and hard—decisions. You can hold on to the idea that you can feel guilt *and* still choose to do something meaningful to you.

TAKING STEPS FORWARD

Many people in therapy get stuck analyzing *why* they feel a certain way, believing once they figure it out, they won't feel this way anymore. But as psychotherapist Lori Gottlieb puts it, finding the reason behind our behavior is like receiving the "booby prize" in therapy: It doesn't change what's actually happening in our lives.[5] Actions, however, will. When you take actions that come from your values, they become positive reinforcers. Because they feel good, you're more likely to do them again. It's the key to breaking free from thought loops and making a decision based on what really matters to you. If you're feeling stuck, try filling in the blanks in this sentence: "In order to uphold the value of [value], I'm willing to [action], even if I feel [anxiety/overwhelm/stress] while doing it."

EMBRACING UNCERTAINTY

Our love for certainty, predictability, and familiarity means that, when making choices, we want to know what the outcome will be. Yet the only thing we can know for certain is that we can't control other people or the outcome of situations. When it comes to living shared values in a relationship, commit to trying what you don't know. If your shared value is connection, then commit to the goal of expressing appreciation every day, even if your partner doesn't remember to return it. If your shared value is family, commit to lunch visits with your in-laws, even if you don't know how they'll go. If your shared value is autonomy, commit to setting a boundary around your in-laws' visits, even if you suspect they'll push back. You don't know what will happen, but you get to make choices. When you commit to living from your shared values, you become a stronger team with your partner, even if it might mean upsetting others.

FINDING A WORKABLE BALANCE

Certain values you hold might be in tension with each other in your day-to-day life. The value of being with your family might clash with the value of advancing your career. The value of supporting your family of origin might conflict with the value of connection with your partner. There's no such thing as complete balance, so instead of striving to achieve 100 percent perfect equilibrium between all values, focus on workability. Remember that values are a guide to help us lead the lives we want to be leading, not a straitjacket.

CHANGE YOUR GOALS, NOT YOUR VALUES

An inevitable truth is that as we pursue a value, we might work toward a goal that ends up being impossible. Let's say your value is cross-generational family connection and your goal is for your MIL to be involved in regular visits with your kids, but she doesn't make these visits even after you've communicated with her about it. Since you can't control your MIL's actions, you'll need to change that goal and find a new way for that value to be met. Maybe you "adopt" an older neighbor as a surrogate grandparent in your family, maybe you and the kids volunteer at a local assisted-living facility, or maybe your value shifts to focus on friends who are your chosen family. There are many ways to surround your kids with loving older adults, even if your MIL isn't very involved. But be sure to reality test and update your goals so that you're not setting yourself up for unmet needs and expectations.

COMMITTING TO WHAT MATTERS
AND LETTING GO OF WHAT DOESN'T

One of Julie's values was connection with Damion, but when she tried to live out that value, she kept getting stuck on her ideas of what "should" happen between families. Sometimes she felt she "should" prioritize her mother-in-law's needs and acquiesce to her frequent requests for Damion's support. After all, she understood Damion's history and could see how important his mother was to him. At other times, she felt she "should" help Damion by pushing him to change the dysfunctional dynamic between him and his mother, since he couldn't seem to do it on his own.

I pressed Julie to consider her values: "I wonder if you could take the time and energy that you're giving to what you think you 'should' be doing and put it toward focusing on what really matters to you." This was something Julie had never considered before. She started to see that she was stuck in a loop between "I must accept that this situation will never improve" and "I must fix this situation single-handedly," neither of which was true. As a result, Julie was wearing herself out and creating more distance from her husband.

Many of us spend our time looking outward and aligning ourselves with others' values. We have a narrative that sounds like "Others prioritize X, so I should too" or "So-and-so says I should be more Y, so I will." But this only leads us to a sense of discontent and greater disconnection from ourselves. The more we look outward, the more we cut off connecting with our authentic selves and with our partners.

Part of aligning with your values is letting go of values that aren't serving you. The process of letting go asks you to bring awareness to who you are and what you struggle with, but it also asks you to identify what lights you up. Ask yourself: What value was behind the last thing you did that brought you joy? How did you decide to do that thing? How did you actually end up doing that thing? What did you have to let go of or not give focus to in order to do that thing?

After bringing awareness to what is important to you, you can start to create separation between you and the obstacle that's holding you back. It might be a thought loop that keeps you stuck or an expectation or desire for others to change. The art of letting go requires us not to stay stuck in our old stories but rather to consciously choose to create a new one.

Damion's journey to creating a more functional relationship with his mother included letting go of the belief that he was solely responsible for her. He had to see that by prioritizing the value of being a "good son" above his value for shared connection and a strong marriage with Julie, he was undermining both relationships. When Damion was honest and clear about his values, without being hooked into the belief that longer summer visits meant a better relationship with his mother (or the belief that his mother would ever stop playing the victim), he was then able to be honest with himself about how long *he* wanted the visits to be.

It's a risk to live aligned with your values—it requires letting go. Letting go of the need to control the outcome. Letting go of the need for others to be happy with you all the time. Letting go of the need to be right. Living aligned asks us to make a commitment every single day to what really matters to us.

During one holiday season, after Julie and Damion had worked with the V step of the VAULT process, Damion's mother started pressuring them to spend more time with her. Instead of launching into their habitual fight, Julie said to Damion, "Let's come back to our values." This acted as a grounding tool for both of them. Julie didn't get stuck on "My MIL needs to stop this behavior" and Damion didn't get stuck on "I need to please my mother." They both wanted to prioritize the value they placed on their relationship, and Damion decided he wanted to do that by spending the holiday at home and making memories with Julie instead of spending extra time with his mother.

After making this choice that aligned with his values, he realized that his mother wasn't any more or less upset than usual. Her issues were with his father and the past, and no matter how hard he tried, nothing he did could fix that. Damion had been chasing an unattainable goal. It didn't matter what he did for her; she would never be able to validate him and express true interest in his life unless she did her own work on healing her wounds from her marriage, which Damion couldn't do for her. From then on, even though he still struggled to let go of the guilt, he turned to Julie to talk about it and recenter himself in their values as a couple instead of reacting from a false sense of responsibility. And the more they returned to their values together, the closer Julie felt to Damion, and the more compassion and patience she was able to extend to her MIL. The following summer they were able to enjoy their time at the vacation home without major arguments because they trusted each other to be on the same page about their values.

This is why simply identifying our values is only the first step. We have to commit to living aligned with them to start making changes. No one can identify your values for you, nor can they tell you how to put your values into practice. You decide how you will intentionally take action toward living out what matters to you.

Once you're well grounded in your values, it's time to move on to the next step in the VAULT method: aspirations. In the next chapter, we're going to talk more about your ideals and desires for a connected and communicative relationship with your MIL.

Chapter 6

ASPIRATIONS

———

Perhaps this has happened to you: You and your husband both knew that you valued your families. In the early days of your relationship, you agreed on visiting your in-laws regularly and having them be a part of you and your kids' lives. You were aligned on what matters, walking life's path side by side. But then, when you got married or had children, something changed. Your mother-in-law became controlling or downright mean to you. Now she tells your husband that she doesn't want you to be part of family events, and when you do attend, you're ignored, belittled, or made to feel like an outsider. You keep attending because you want to be a "we" with your husband, but after each visit, you feel smaller and more invisible.

Or maybe your MIL is supportive and open, but your husband insists on visiting her every Sunday for four hours, the most inconvenient time for you as you need to prepare for the week ahead. You're confident your MIL would be flexible about skipping a weekend now and then, and you try to find alternatives with your husband, but he insists family time is important—even though you suspect he simply feels guilty saying no.

In both of these scenarios, you and your husband were in agreement about your values, but when it came to actually applying those values, things began to derail. This is because a shared commitment to the value of family doesn't automatically translate to mutually satisfying actions taken as partners. It's one thing to say, "We value family." It's another to say, "We value family, *and therefore* we aren't visiting my mother when she treats my wife badly."

In the last chapter, we discussed the first step in the VAULT method: values. In this chapter, we'll discuss aspirations—the goals you want to set and the specific actions you aim to take based on those values. We'll explore how you and your husband may not currently be living up to your values, how to disrupt these behaviors, and how to help you both have clear expectations for a shared future moving forward.

DISRUPTING DYSFUNCTION

Let's revisit Carly, whom we met in chapter 1. She and her husband, Nigel, had recently had their first baby, a boy. But every Sunday at her in-laws' home, her mother-in-law would make some version of the same toxic comment out of her son's earshot: "You're just a distraction to my son. You aren't my grandson's real family." Even more confounding for Carly, Nigel refused to believe that his mother was making such hateful comments, or to stand up for Carly and their family of three.

As Carly's resentment built, her MIL was successfully making her an outsider. At family events, Nigel would turn a cold shoulder to Carly, avoiding eye contact with her while profusely complimenting his mother's appearance and cooking. On the drive home, Carly would try to get him to see how painful the experience had been, but he would only tell her it wasn't a big deal, leaving Carly to wonder: Is this okay? Am I overreacting? And what should I do?

I want to talk about Nigel's reactions to his mother because this will help us understand the next step in changing the dynamic. Without identifying your husband's reactive behavior, you'll remain cycling through the same events with no new outcome. My clients stuck in this cycle ask the same questions: Why isn't my husband seeing this? Why doesn't he stand up for me? Why doesn't he stand up for us? Why is nothing changing?

In triggering moments with our families, we can all default to outdated coping strategies if we haven't consciously learned to recognize the triggers and choose new responses. For adult sons, these strategies commonly include going on autopilot, compartmentalization, falling into a guilt-shame spiral, all-or-nothing thinking, and avoidance. All of these strategies aim to protect them from having to experience difficult feelings in response to their mother's actions. These strategies were effective enough when they were navigating their relationship with their mother by themselves, but they become inadequate when a partner and/or children enter the picture.

If this is what you're going through, remember, your husband and his mother had their dynamic before you joined the family. All you're doing is disrupting their patterns, and if those patterns were dysfunctional, that's actually a good thing. But in the short term, it can leave you feeling that you're not on the same page with your husband and are disconnected from the future you aspire to share with him. But before we talk about the aspirations we have for healthier coping strategies, we have to look at one of the main factors keeping us stuck in the unhealthy ones: a dysregulated nervous system.

YOUR NERVOUS SYSTEM

The good news is that you and your husband can learn to identify when you're using unhealthy coping strategies and build new, healthier strategies to help you break the cycle and take action. This requires looking at your nervous system and how your body is reacting to your environment. Yes, your body. Your mind and body are intimately interconnected, and we need to familiarize ourselves with both to shift what is happening between you, your husband, and your mother-in-law.

My favorite aha moment in my own work came from discovering this expression: Story follows state.[1] We often assume that in order to make our bodies feel calm, we need to control our thoughts—that is, we think that if we have negative thoughts running through our brains, this causes unpleasant feelings in our body. In reality, it's often the other way around: The narratives we tell ourselves are the *result* of the state of our bodies. This is because your amygdala, the almond-shaped structure in the back of your brain responsible for emotion, senses information and threat at a rapid speed, and it sends messages to your body well before your prefrontal cortex (which controls your logic and higher-order thinking) can come in to assess the threat. The body's reaction comes *before* the mind's.

We can understand what happens in your body by looking at the four states our nervous system can enter when it encounters a perceived threat. The threat doesn't have to be physical or even completely concrete; even a sense of uncertainty might feel like a threat to the amygdala, triggering your prefrontal cortex to start spinning negative narratives. As you read, remember, the goal is not to avoid experiencing these states, which would be impossible—they happen in our bodies faster than we can think. The goal is to be able to bring awareness to the state you're in so you can respond more intentionally to what is happening in hard moments with your husband or MIL.

The four states are:

* **Fight:** In fight mode, you react to a perceived threat by confronting it head-on, often feeling aggression and anger. You might become argumentative, maybe even controlling. Fight mode makes us feel more at ease by letting us focus outward and try to control the situation. Common signs of being in fight mode include a tight jaw, a racing heart,

anger, irritability, the urge to hit or stomp, and increased body temperature.

* **Flight:** In flight mode, you want to flee from the perceived threat—but that doesn't always mean physically removing yourself from the situation. People find ways to mentally escape the threat through strategies like perfectionism, compartmentalization, or distracting themselves with work or other activities in an effort to avoid what's happening in front of them. Common signs of being in flight mode include fidgeting, restlessness, irritability, anxiety, feeling tense or trapped, constant movement, and an urge for high-exertion exercise.

* **Freeze:** Freezing is a sense of feeling stuck, with an inability to make decisions, take action, or change patterns. People often feel numb, depressed, and flat when frozen. Many also talk about dissociating from reality. Common signs include dread, feeling chilled or cold, feeling hyperalert or tense, increased heart rate, dizziness, apathy, and minimal verbal responses.

* **Fawn:** When people "fawn" in response to a perceived threat, they are likely to people please, subjugate their own wants and needs, lose their identity and boundaries, feel overwhelmed, and engage in codependent behaviors. Children often learn this response in a household that contains physical abuse, emotional neglect, or inconsistent nurturing, in an attempt to win over a cold or critical parent. (Carly realized that Nigel tried to cope with his mother's behavior first by fawning and then, if the situation escalated, by freezing.) Common signs of fawning include overagreement, self-subjugation, concern with others' happiness at the expense of your own, exhaustion, losing boundaries, and feeling controlled.

Practice noticing the different states that you experience throughout the day, outside of high-emotion events that might arise with your MIL. For example, when I've been writing for long periods of time, my nervous system can slip into a freeze state as I stare at a blank page. Or when the kids are running up and down the hall at bedtime, my fight state might start to kick in. It's my job to bring in tools like the ones in the next section to help me return to a place of calm regulation. This practice is helpful for preparing for those hard moments with your MIL.

REGULATING THE NERVOUS SYSTEM

When your nervous system is dysregulated, it can feel like you go on autopilot. But once you start to recognize what states you—and your husband—default to, you can start disrupting any un-helpful coping mechanisms that have become second nature when you enter fight, flight, freeze, or fawn modes. Learning to respond to difficult situations from a regulated nervous system is an important aspiration to aim for. In stressful moments, you can learn to soothe your nervous system using tools like physical movements, breath work, and mental imagery.

Because fight and flight modes are associated with a *hyper-*activated nervous system, you can regulate by *decreasing* your nervous system's activation. Here are some possible tools to help disrupt these states:

* Label anger and irritability out loud.

* Turn off screens, which can be overstimulating.

* Call to mind or look at a picture of a calm scene or place you felt safe in.

* Practice gentle movement (e.g., a walk around the block, a gentle yoga flow).

* Hum or sing out loud.

* Stand outside and look up.

* Lie on the floor with your legs extended up the wall.

* Try a weighted blanket or deep pressure hug.

* Shake your hands while moving your arms up and down.

* Tense various body parts and then release them (this is called progressive muscular relaxation).

Freeze and fawn modes are the opposite; they're associated with a *hypo*activated (shut down) nervous system, so you can help regulate by *increasing* your nervous system's activation. Here are some tools to do so:

* Dance.

* Bounce up and down on a trampoline or just on your heels.

* Skip or do "high knees."

* Do push-ups.

* Listen to music.

* Roll like a ball on the ground.

* Do grounding exercises (e.g., notice five things you can see, four things you can touch, three things you can hear, two things you can smell or taste, and one slow deep breath).

* Do a safe-place meditation.

* Do a box-breathing exercise (breathe in for a count of four, hold for a count of four, breathe out for a count of four, hold for a count of four, and repeat).

UNDERSTANDING INDIVIDUATION

In addition to noticing when your nervous system is dysregulated and practicing bringing it back into regulation, there is another key component to shifting out of autopilot and into living the healthy relationship you aspire to with both your partner and your MIL. That component is individuation.

What is individuation, and how is it different from the process of differentiation I touched on in chapter 4? Whereas differentiation is the process of gradually achieving healthy separation from your family, individuation is about defining your sense of self: who you are, what you like, and what you don't like. According to family therapist Dr. Murray Bowen, people who are more individuated have less emotional reactivity and better objectivity to see their family dynamics for what they are.[2]

Technically speaking, you have been individuating your whole life. Babies first begin to recognize that they're separate from their caregivers at around four months old. An eight-month-old can be seen practicing individuation by pushing away their caregivers to indicate that they don't want a hug or are ready to be put down to explore their environment. Toddlers regularly yell, "No!," and assert what they want—or don't want! This is a normal process and developmentally appropriate. However, when caregivers are not able to view their child as separate from them, or when there are other toxic family dynamics (as discussed in chapter 2), the separation between caregiver and child is stunted and the children are not allowed to become their own individual selves.

Even as a teenager, my client Simon would come home wanting space from his parents, but his mother insisted on talking about his day as soon as he got in the door. When his mother hovered over him while he was trying to complete tasks, he often felt frustrated, wanting to tell her to just let him figure it out. His mother had trouble letting him individuate and grow into his own person, and today he struggles to identify his own needs and defaults to people-pleasing. His mother's own parents probably had trouble letting her individuate when she was young; family members struggle more with others' boundaries and individuation if they themselves are not individuated.

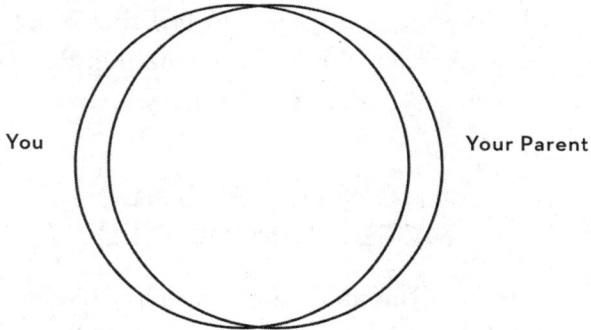

Without healthy individuation, there is not enough separation between you and your parent. In this enmeshed dynamic, you are expected to have the same thoughts, feelings, beliefs, opinions, desires, and needs as your parent.

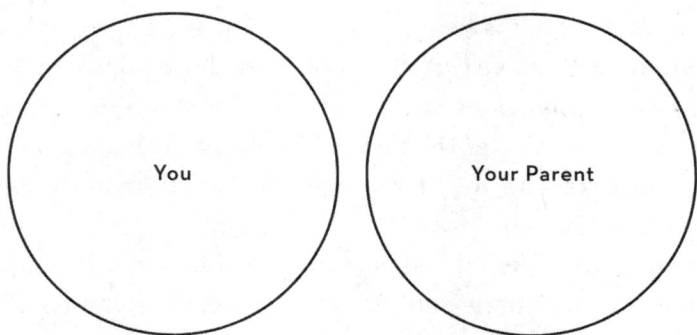

When there is healthy individuation between you and your parent, you each have your own separate thoughts, feelings, beliefs, opinions, desires, and needs.

Individuation is important to helping you build your own family as an adult. When you enter into a long-term committed relationship, you're both choosing to leave behind the family as you knew it. The goal isn't to cut people out. Instead, you're discerning which parts of your values and ways of being you will bring forward to create a new family unit. With the goal of building your autonomy, you and your husband want to focus on your own beliefs, with a willingness and openness to change repeating cycles and let go of old, unhelpful behaviors.

Naturally, this process of individuation can create tension in both your families of origin. This experience may be uncomfortable, but it's actually quite normal to feel that sense of friction between members when they're individuating. Remember, tension is an opportunity for growth for everyone.

HOW TO BECOME
MORE INDIVIDUATED

Now I want to help you apply the concept of individuation in a concrete way. Note that, while I'm going to address this to you, the daughter-in-law, this work requires both partners, so you can invite your partner to read this section too.

The first step requires you to bring awareness to the moments you go on autopilot. Recognize what is happening in your environment, what is being said, and what you are experiencing in your body. Practice getting out of these dysregulated states, as discussed in a previous section of this chapter. Sometimes this awareness comes after the fact, which is totally normal; it's one of the ways you can start learning to do something different the next time it happens.

The second step of individuation requires you to build acceptance of the family you've married into. Acceptance doesn't mean you like your family's behavior or choices; rather, it means you simply see it for what it is. I like to use the concept of radical acceptance, which, according to psychologist Tara Brach, means recognizing what you're feeling in the present moment with compassion, without judging or criticizing.[3] You aren't resisting what you're experiencing or trying to tell yourself that his family should change or that your partner should do anything differently. You're not in the past or the future. You have an openness for seeing what is happening in this moment as it is.

Acceptance for your MIL might sound like "My feelings are valid, *and* I'm letting go of trying to change her," or "I'm not getting my needs met," or "These are her choices." If you want to borrow motivational speaker Mel Robbins's phrasing, you could say "let them"—let them be the way they are.[4] These statements aren't necessarily comforting, but they help you stop resisting a desire to change things you can't personally change. My go-to acceptance strategy is to practice "dropping the rope." In this case the rope represents the struggle you get into in your mind arguing why other people should be different. If you put the rope down, you are no longer wasting energy dragging against something out of your control.

The third step of individuation requires you to detach your MIL's feelings about you from who you are as a person. When she projects her feelings onto you, that's her coping mechanism. It's intended to make her feelings yours so that you're the one feeling guilt or shame instead of her. Recognize that her emotions do not mean anything about your worthiness. One of the ways you can remind yourself of that is by practicing statements like the following:

* I am a good person.

* I am enough and worthy.

* My feelings are just as important as my MIL's.

* I don't need to meet every one of my MIL's needs, *and* I am still a lovable person.

The fourth step of individuation is to disentangle yourself from the unhelpful messages and beliefs that you have absorbed without realizing it. This will require you to boldly find your own ways of thinking about family, relationships, childrearing, and connection rather than defaulting to rules you believe you "should" or "have to" adhere to because of a sense of guilt or pressure from your family.

The final step requires a much harder and ongoing process: grief. When you practice acceptance for your families and the toxic dynamics that exist, you also mourn several things: who you wanted them to be, who they won't be for you or for your children, and your hopes and dreams for what "family" would look like that didn't come to fruition. You've probably heard of the five stages of grief: denial, anger, bargaining, depression, and acceptance (and a sixth stage added by David Kessler, finding meaning).[5] A popular misconception is that everyone progresses through the stages in that order and then arrives at the end, moving on from grief for good. In reality, you will likely find yourself moving back and forth between stages and experiencing more than one at a time. You'll feel acceptance one day and anger on another. Be patient with yourself. Grief is not linear, and in some ways, it will always be with you, even as you live a meaningful and fulfilling life.

As Simon worked to individuate from his family and step out of his pattern of going into freeze mode, he found himself cycling through the stages of grief. At times, he'd be in a state of denial, searching for ways to prove that his mother was a good parent. Then he'd slip into anger at her for all his childhood hurts. Then, through periods of acceptance, he'd see his mother for who she really was: a woman unable to meet his needs. Simon's work included understanding and accepting his stages of grief, and building meaningful connections with other people in his life to create a family by choice.

A DESIRED FUTURE
AND A SHARED VISION

It's now time to move from the 35,000-foot view of individuation to a more granular look at your day-to-day aspirations as a couple.

In chapter 5, I touched on how couples often say they were initially on the same page about values, but when it came time to live out those values, things got derailed. I commonly hear couples say things like "We talked about how we valued family visits, but we never talked about the length of the visits, where people would stay, how long they would stay, or what we'd do when we had a baby." When I polled my online community, 80 percent of people indicated that they did not make an explicit list of expectations or desires before getting married, about how they planned to navigate communication, connection, or their general relationship with their mother-in-law. One exception was the person who told me that having these conversations before getting married almost broke their relationship, but that years later they continue to be on the same page. I believe it is never too late to have this type of conversation.

Couples struggle to get on the same page, often because they haven't had conversations about their shared desires. In the following exercise, we're going to look at just that: openly discussing what you want to happen between you, your husband, and his mother.

As you work through the questions, make sure to consider how the strengths and challenges of your DIL style might contribute to how you answer these questions and co-create with your partner. This will also help you choose what to focus on in getting on the same page as your partner.

DIL STYLE	STRENGTHS	
Good Girl	Caring Puts others first Compassionate Able to recognize others' feelings Flexible Accommodating to others' needs and wishes	
Manager	Has certainty Places high value on routine Protects time and family's well-being Plans	
Balancer	Brings people together Healthy boundaries Flexible and accommodating Consciously chooses where to put energy	

CHALLENGES	WHAT TO FOCUS ON
Porous boundaries Self-abandonment tendencies Ignores connection to sense of self Lives in regret and turmoil from not asserting self	Think of your needs first. Remind yourself that your worth comes from within, not from pleasing others. Go slow when responding. Try to have a hard inside (firm boundary), soft outside (empathic approach).
Rigid boundaries Wavering sense of self when feeling uncertainty or loss of control Inflexible to others' wishes and needs	Practice looking at the bigger picture over the minutiae. Ask more questions and listen with curiosity to understand your partner. Put the value of connection with family at the same priority as the value of boundaries.
Overcommits to one value over another Overfocuses on "we" and loses individual "I" Gets frustrated when others don't see situations with nuance	Practice prioritizing your autonomy and seeing the long-term benefits. Allow others to own tasks if this becomes burdensome. Accept MIL for who she is. Grieve MIL if she is not the desired in-law you had hoped for.

Exercise:

Your Shared Desires

The following questions should help you and your partner uncover your similarities and differences and make a plan you can
share moving forward on a variety of topics. Remember, this is
an inventory, not a cause for conflict or defensiveness. If you
don't understand your partner's response or start feeling defensive, get curious and ask them to tell you more or describe how
they see this unfolding. If you get stuck, return to chapter 4 to
get out of your negative cycle and implement those healthy communication tools.

Connection

* Who will be responsible for making plans with your family?

* Who will be responsible for maintaining the connection
  with your family?

* Who will be purchasing gifts for your family? How much
  will we spend?

* How do you want to approach group texts with your family?

* How often will we see your family?

* How long will our visits be?

* How much notice do we need before a visit?

* How do we determine when a visit is over?

* Who will we stay with when we visit?

* How do we navigate reciprocity with traveling? When do we want to go to them, and when do we want them to come to us?

* If your family/MIL is in the hospital or ill, who is responsible for arranging visits?

* Do you expect our parents to be friends? Connected in some way?

Communication

* What is your ideal for who will communicate with your mother?

* If your mother texts me for information, how will I respond?

* What information do you feel is appropriate to share with your mother? What information do you feel is not appropriate to share with your mother?

* When we have a disagreement about our needs and your mother's wishes, what should we do to handle it?

* What will we do if your mother calls/texts me because you don't call/text her?

* When we hit hard moments in our life (e.g., work stress, unemployment, mental health, infertility, my own family challenges), how would we like to address this with your family? Who shares this information, and what information is shared?

Family Roles

* What role will your mother play in our marriage?

* What role do you foresee/desire your mother having when we have children?

* What role do you want your mother to play when it comes to our own marital conflict?

* What role will you and I play when your parents age? When they need assisted living and more support?

* What role will you and I play when one of your parents passes away?

* If your mother lives with us, what role does she play in our home? With the kids?

* If your mother lives with us, how can we create boundaries for separate time (e.g., arranging shared or separate dinnertimes, creating shared and separate spaces)?

Your Parenthood Journey

* Who do we want to be present at the birth of our child(ren)?

* After having a baby, when do we want family to visit?

* How long do we want them to stay?

* How involved do we want them to be?

* Do we feel comfortable having them care for our baby? What limits are there?

* At what age will we feel comfortable leaving our baby with your mother to babysit?

* At what age can our children have an overnight stay at their grandparents'?

* What will we do with unsolicited parenting advice?

* How will we approach unhelpful comments from grandparents about our parenting decisions?

* How will we approach grandparents buying gifts for our kids?

* What decisions do we want to make about family using alcohol/substances around our kids?

* How will we approach well-meaning but unwanted touch/hugs/kisses (e.g., when a grandparent directs a child to "come say goodbye properly with a hug")?

* If I am sick, how will we decide if your mother is the right person to assist you with the home and kids?

Conflict

* How do you want to handle conflict with your mother?

* Who will set boundaries with your mother?

* What does it mean to stand up for each other?

* Who sets boundaries when/if family overstays during a visit?

* What will you do if your mother is disrespectful to me? To the kids?

* What will you do if you hit hard moments in your relationship with your mother and your own childhood trauma?

* How do we handle hurtful comments and behavior from your mother?

* What will we do if I'm having a hard time with something your mother does or says and you're not?

* How will you continue to portray me in a positive light to your mother?

* If your parents don't meet our desires/wishes (e.g., they don't visit as often as we'd like them to), what will we do?

* If you are in a difficult phase with your mother, does that apply to me? The kids?

* How do we want to handle sibling rivalry insofar as it involves your parents and impacts our family?

* How do we want to handle when we are in disagreement about any of the above (e.g., therapy, couples therapy, or mediation)?

Finances

* Do you foresee helping your parents financially?

* How will we decide whether to help them, how much to help them, and for how long?

* Do you see your parents helping us financially, and on what conditions would we accept the help?

* How do we want to accept/receive financial support should we need it?

* If your parents own our property or have lent us another significant item like a car, what plans do we need to make to protect our own finances should something change?

Religion and Culture

* What are our cultural differences, and how do we want to approach these?

* What cultural values might your mother hold that perhaps we don't want in our relationship?

* What traditions are essential in our chosen family that come from our culture and religion?

* If we have two different backgrounds/religions, how will we integrate them into our family?

* What role will your family play in nurturing religion with us and/or with the kids?

* Who will communicate our choices regarding our participation in religion?

Holidays/Events

* What desires do you have around holidays with our families of origin?

* How will this change when we have our own kids?

* How do we want to split our time on holidays between families?

* Your mother will have expectations about holidays. What are our desires and wishes for family events?

* How far in advance are we willing to plan holidays?

* As our children grow, who decides what holidays and events we can miss? What will we do if your parents have expectations that are different from our wishes?

Questions to Help You Set Your Desires Together

Answer these questions individually.

* What do I want to bring to this relationship?

* What am I willing to compromise on, knowing that this matters to my partner?

* What are my nonnegotiables?

* What "I require . . ." statements can I make in a way that works for both me and my husband?

Answer these questions together.

* How do you envision a life together with family?

* How important is this specific issue to you?

* What are some of the themes that we're noticing in our answers?

* If we disagree on a specific topic from any part of this exercise, what could each of us do to solve it? What would this require of you? What would it require of me?

* Looking at all your desires, what is the top one that is nonnegotiable?

* What did you like that your parents did while growing up that you would like to continue?

* Thinking of the things your parents do (or did when you were a child) that you don't like, what do you want to avoid doing in our family?

* Looking at all the questions in this exercise, instead of trying to be in complete agreement on all of them, what are the top five issues that come up for us as a family, and how can we find solutions and common ground on those?

FROM GRIDLOCK TO COMPROMISE

When it comes to identifying our relationship desires, I want you to hold in mind that no two people feel the same way about everything, especially when it comes to family. I often think that co-creating with a partner is like playing in a sandbox. If I tell my husband that he can't bring trucks and cars into the sandbox and that we *only* play with shovels and buckets, the space is only defined by me. That isn't a relationship. But if I make space for him to make roads and parking garages while still having designated areas for my castles, we create a relationship that works for both of us. This is my favorite analogy for what it means to practice two key principles in relationships: accepting influence and building compromise.

Too often, couples can get stuck in a zero-sum approach. When making decisions around important topics, one person aims to win, which results in the other person losing. Of course, no one wants to be "the loser," so both partners dig in their heels instead of engaging in give-and-take.

For couples who get stuck in this kind of gridlock, power is an important factor to consider. Power negotiations occur in the small daily decisions we make (e.g., what's for dinner, which TV show you're going to watch), but they also occur in bigger decisions like where you'll live and how you'll spend the holidays. When people lose power, they end up feeling small, disconnected, and resentful. The solution is focusing on meeting the needs of the "we" and not the individual "I." Remember, you're playing doubles tennis. You're on the same team, and you want the team to win, not a single individual.

Psychologist Dan Wile said it best: "When choosing a long-term partner, you will inevitably be choosing a particular set of unsolvable problems that you'll be grappling with for the next ten, twenty or fifty years."[6] In fact, in their Love Lab research, Drs. John and Julie Gottman found that *most* problems—69 percent—are perpetual, which means that it's imperative to come up with solutions that don't result in either partner abandoning their wants and needs.[7]

One powerful approach to navigating conflict and differences is *accepting influence*. Couples who allow themselves to be influenced by each other are more likely to remain together and report feeling connected in long-term studies. The Gottmans found that men in heterosexual marriages who allowed their wives to influence them were more likely to be in happy long-term relationships, while men who refused to share decision-making with their wives had an 81 percent probability of separation.[8]

What does it mean to accept influence? It means remaining open to understanding what your partner desires and where these desires come from. It means viewing your position as flexible. It doesn't mean you collapse and fold into the other person. You don't lose yourself. Instead, it means holding openness toward your partner and being willing to change your position on the issue at hand.

However, I also want to say that I have heard your MIL stories. They're painful, and many of you have been treated terribly. If you have a desire to dig in your heels, I get it. But digging in your heels ultimately might not be what's best for the greater good of your relationship or your personal happiness. It's why we're using the aspirations step of the VAULT system to help you find what's going to be workable. Stay with me!

Which brings me to the next piece: the art of compromise. Compromise is about finding areas of flexibility within what is inflexible. Compromise is not about abandoning what is important to you, nor is it about continuing to point out all the ways in which your partner should change. These positions keep you in gridlock or push you toward the zero-sum approach. A true compromise comes from finding what feels workable for both people.

To start the compromise process, you'll want to identify your areas of inflexibility, or your core needs. I introduced core needs and longings in chapter 4 when we looked at your negative communication cycle. Core needs are like the lights on the runway, directing the airplane where to land—they guide you and your partner on what actions to take. Needs come from within us and are connected to our values, desires, and identity. Identifying and expressing needs helps us understand each other better and build a stronger connection.

I know identifying your core needs can be challenging, so here are some tips to help you do so. Over time and with practice, identifying needs does become easier, even for those who have little practice doing it.

* Make space for self-reflection. Trying to identify a need in a moment when emotions are high will likely result in anger and your ego needing to be right.

* Ask yourself, "What do I need?" or "What do I need to feel safe and connected right now?" Listen to the first answer that shows up for you. You could also take the response and see how it fits in the categories of the eight core relational needs (see pages 79–83 in chapter 4).

* Explore your feelings first, then see what need comes up. In chapter 4, I talked about identifying the primary core emotion underneath the secondary emotion. This is a great place to begin when it comes to identifying needs. Start by naming your emotion and seeing what the emotion leads you to need. For example: "I feel sad. When I feel sad, it's helpful for me to . . ." or "I feel scared and uncertain. This feeling needs . . ."

* Sometimes identifying what you *don't* want can help you see your need. For example: "I don't need connection and play right now. I need more freedom and autonomy." Or: "Being more autonomous right now isn't helping me feel grounded. I need validation."

Once you and your partner can determine your respective core needs, which are inflexible, you can then start to look at the areas that *are* flexible. When it comes to looking for flexibility, you're looking at ways in which this goal could be fulfilled. When discussing your MIL, focus on what is important for each of you and not necessarily what your MIL can or can't do, what she desires of you, or how you want her to change.

Carly and Nigel were at a standstill about how they wanted to approach his mother. Carly couldn't tolerate her MIL's verbal abuse anymore and was firm on the couple not going to her house until she changed. Nigel, on the other side, believed being with family was a nonnegotiable—and that staying connected with his mother was important. The problem was that they were coming from completely different perspectives. Carly's area of inflexibility was her core need to feel like she had some power and choice over how she was treated and what she was exposed to. Nigel's area of inflexibility was about being connected with his mother. Only after identifying these areas of inflexibility were they able to start exploring the areas where they did overlap or could find ways to do so moving forward.

Exercise:

Questions for Compromise

Ask each other the following questions (adapted from the work of Drs. John and Julie Gottman) to find a solution that works for both of you.[9] First you will identify your areas of inflexibility and then your areas of potential compromise. But remember, if you're asking your partner to play in your sandbox using only buckets and shovels, you are not co-creating.

Questions to Help Find Areas of Inflexibility

* What is my core need/area of inflexibility for this issue?

* What is my partner's core need/area of inflexibility for this issue?

* What makes my core need so important to me? How did this come to be in my life?

* What areas within this am I absolutely not willing to bend on?

Questions to Help Find Areas of Flexibility

* What areas of this am I willing to be flexible on? For how long, where, and when?

* What emotions come up when I think about having this need met? Not having it met?

* What do I need you to understand about this core need/ area of inflexibility?

* What desires do we have in common when it comes to this situation?

* What would it mean to let go of this need for twenty-four hours?

* How might you and I find a middle ground on what we both want?

* If I were living a meaningful life, two years from now, feeling joy and connection, how important would this be to me?

When completing this exercise, Carly discovered that Nigel had a deep fear of losing his parents and that he often felt like Carly was trying to take him away from them. Carly was able to empathize with just how important family was to him and affirm that she loved his commitment to his community and family. Meanwhile, Nigel discovered that Carly's need to feel a sense of power and choice stemmed from growing up in a highly controlling household. In exploring this, they found parts of each other that they hadn't seen before, and this opened up an entirely new conversation.

As their son grew older, Carly felt more comfortable with Nigel taking him to her MIL's place without her, and Nigel agreed to make these visits shorter. This compromise meant that Nigel got to see his family and that Carly had a choice in whether she participated. Moving forward, Carly opted out of the casual "drop-ins" and weekly meals Nigel would have with his family. For holidays or special events, Carly was willing to attend a time-limited gathering if Nigel agreed to not leave her side around his mother.

Although initially Nigel felt that he was being "tied" to his wife, he was able to soften and agree to trying this approach so that they could still have contact with his family. Carly and Nigel found solutions when they began to step out of their all-or-nothing thinking about family involvement and found a new approach.

Exercise:
Getting Unstuck

It's common for people to get stuck when looking for a compromise because of the story we're telling ourselves. This story might be "I'm being asked to be the victim" or "I'm always made out to be the bad guy." Maybe you're rehashing old events with your MIL, reliving hurts and resentments. Use this two-minute exercise to get into a more compassionate mindset. Compassion brings understanding. With understanding, we are more likely to make decisions from a place of empathy and curiosity.

Take five slow deep breaths in and out through your nose. If you're finding it difficult to focus on your breath, place one hand on your heart and one on your abdomen. Feel your hands rise and fall as you ground yourself in your breath. On your sixth breath, ask yourself, "How am I getting trapped inside my mind?"

Listen for a moment to see what shows up for you. As you continue breathing, now ask, "How is my partner seeming to get stuck in his mind?"

With your next breath, bring a statement of compassion to yourself. Think of what you would say to a dear friend struggling in this moment. You might say, "It makes sense that you're struggling" or "You're not alone in this struggle."

Now, bring a statement of compassion to your partner. Think of what you would say from a place of tenderness if you were sitting in front of a younger version of your partner. You might say, "I see that this is hard for you" or "You're doing your best right now."

By reconnecting with your partner, even if only in your mind, you're creating a shared moment of peace. Sometimes that's enough to shift the energy of the whole conflict.

Carly and Nigel began to feel a new sense of connection once they identified their aspirations and compromised on what visits with his mother entailed. Carly's work in therapy also focused on helping her strengthen her inner trust that, no matter what her MIL said, Nigel had chosen her to build a life with. Carly also started to see that despite her MIL's negative remarks, Carly's role as a mother to her own son was essential. She didn't need to fear losing her son to her MIL, as she was the primary parent helping him to build security and to feel seen and soothed. This sense of empowerment helped her to trust not only herself but also Nigel when he spent time with his mother when Carly wasn't there. While Carly's MIL never changed, Carly and Nigel did. They got on the same team.

Now that you've found your shared aspirations and identified areas of influence and compromise that will help you get on the same page, it's time to move on to the next step of the VAULT method and bring awareness to the triangle that exists between you, your husband, and his mother.

Chapter 7

UNDERSTANDING YOUR TRIANGLE

‎

Y‎ou put me in the middle again!" Vanessa yelled. She and her husband, Marcus, were sitting far apart from each other on my couch, both with their arms crossed.

"*I put you* in the middle?" Marcus said. "You're the one who kept telling me that I had to say something to my mom when I didn't even see an issue."

"You never reply to your mother's texts," Vanessa said. "That leaves me in the middle facilitating your whole relationship. She literally asked me the other day if you were eating enough."

They'd had long-standing issues with his mother criticizing Vanessa's ability to "take care of" Marcus, even though they were both grown adults. When Marcus did something his mother didn't like, such as not responding to her texts, she blamed Vanessa, making her the scapegoat for any problems. Instead of setting boundaries with his mother or taking responsibility for communicating with her, Marcus simply avoided dealing with the issue and did nothing, making Vanessa feel she was always stuck in the middle of the conflict between him and his mother.

Marcus, however, felt that Vanessa always put him the middle by trying to force him to set boundaries. From his point of view, asserting his desire to have more space would be starting conflict with his mother. He saw the current conflict as something between Vanessa and his mother that he didn't want to be involved in.

Who is in the middle? It's a question I'm frequently asked, because the couple assumes that once they can figure this out, they can identify who needs to change.

I told Vanessa and Marcus something I tell many couples: "You're both in the middle. Actually, you're in a triangle."

After Values and Aspirations, the next step in the VAULT method is Understanding Your Triangle. This is a critical step, and there's a reason I save it for third. Starting with the triangle can lead people to become defensive and shut down, especially if they don't feel seen and understood. The first two steps focus on building an understanding and a strong "we"-ness as a couple, enabling the emotional safety between partners that's required to resolve hard issues. Now that you've done the work of figuring out your values and aspirations, you're ready to tackle this next step.

But before you start, a word of caution. When you're growing up, your emotional survival hinges on accepting the way your family system operates. While your experiences might not be what others experience or even what's healthy, they are your "normal." When you create a new family, you have the opportunity to decide for yourself what works and what doesn't. But this is challenging because we often don't consciously see the patterns and dynamics we've come from—they just seem normal to us. Remember, the VAULT method is about creating a new kind of relationship. You're exploring yourself as an individual and establishing new patterns as a couple. Understanding is necessary—without it, we can't move forward.

HOW TRIANGLES WORK

A triangle is one of the most common dynamics I see among partners and a mother-in-law. Dr. Murray Bowen, psychiatrist and creator of family systems therapy, coined the term *triangulation* to describe these three-way dynamics that occur in families.[1] As I mentioned in chapter 2, triangulation is a process in which a two-person relationship that is experiencing tension brings in a third person in an attempt to provide balance or stability to the system. When things are pleasant and each person is getting their needs met, triangles often don't occur. We bring in "a third" when a dyad is experiencing stress, anxiety, uncertainty, conflict, or other difficult circumstances. If the relationship between two people is not stable, the triangle will temporarily provide that stability by defusing the tension between the dyad one way or another.

We get stuck in triangles for many of the reasons we touched on in part I. There might be preexisting dynamics in your husband's family that contribute to you being considered an outsider. Your husband might play roles in the family that make it hard for him to set boundaries or assert your needs as a couple, including being a rescuer or the "good child." Communication from your MIL might involve passive-aggressive comments or guilt-tripping remarks that leave you both unable to respond to her. There might also be power struggles, with your MIL wanting to exert some kind of control over you or the family.

However, your MIL and husband aren't the only ones contributing to the triangle. You, too, play a role in it. What role you play depends on how you approach communication with your partner, your desires related to your in-laws, and your expectations and beliefs about what a relationship between mother-in-law and daughter-in-law should be. This is important to remember because we usually enter into triangles unconsciously, trying to alleviate the anxiety and stress we feel without thinking through what the involvement of a third person really means.

Even in a positive MIL-DIL relationship, there is still a risk of stepping into a triangle. This is what happened for Alexandra, who received well-intentioned texts from her Supporter MIL asking how she could help her son during his big job transition.

Alexandra empathized with her MIL's feelings and intentions but informed her that these questions would be best directed to her son. Since they had a healthy relationship, her MIL understood this and texted her son the next day to check in with him instead, successfully stepping out of the triangle.

There's a catch to a triangle: Bringing in a third person only temporarily lowers anxiety and distress. Because it doesn't address the real issues between the primary pair, in the long run, it actually creates *more* turmoil among all three people. There could be a breakdown of trust between husband and wife, for example, or a son and mother could lose the mutuality and respect required to maintain their bond.

Triangles also lead to ongoing power imbalances. Power can be exerted through big decisions (e.g., deciding where to live) or small ones (e.g., deciding what takeout to order one night). Balanced expressions of power are essential to building healthy relationships. In a triangle, one or more people end up feeling a loss of power. Perhaps your MIL feels powerless and uses manipulation or gaslighting with you or your partner to try to exert control. Your husband might be resisting confronting her because he wants to feel like he has power over his own actions and can't be forced into doing something. Or you might be trying to maintain your power by holding inflexible boundaries.

Remember, the actions of all three people in the triangle are part of what is creating the drama. This is why I don't view anyone as being "in the middle" but instead look at the pressure or tension that is put on each person as a result of the three-way dynamic.

Let's explore some examples of triangles.

ANGELA AND JOHN

When they got married after three years together, Angela and John moved into a house that his parents had previously held as a rental property. A place to live seemed like a generous offer at first, but there were strings attached. The deed remained in his parents' names, and they expected to approve every decision about the renovation necessitated by years of rough treatment from tenants. Angela quickly realized that she wasn't being "given" a house—or even the opportunity to buy a house. She was her MIL's tenant, with no more say than any other tenant.

When John got the text that his mother had chosen a paint color they'd vetoed, Angela could see steam coming out of his ears. In an effort to be on his side, she asked, "What do you think about the color?"

But rather than owning his disappointment and frustration at his mother, John picked up on Angela's irritation and turned against his wife: "It's my mom, Angela! I trust her opinion. You would do the same if your mom picked something out." John's defensiveness completely invalidated Angela's feelings.

Leaning toward the Collaborator DIL style in the early days of her relationship with John, Angela had taken extra care to involve her in-laws. But when her opinions were consistently ignored, she felt disrespected. She didn't want to rock the boat, but at the same time, she felt hurt when her MIL treated her like an outsider. Because of this distance, she'd turn to her husband in hopes he'd tackle the issues. This resulted in the tension she felt with her MIL being placed between her and her husband. The following triangle was the result.

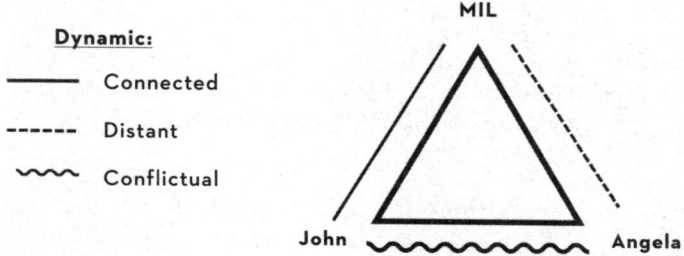

There is conflict between John and Angela, distance between Angela and her MIL, and connection between John and his mother.

CLARISSA AND JASON

When Clarissa started dating Jason, her Good Girl DIL style went into overdrive trying to please his disapproving evangelical family. Although she wasn't a practicing Christian, she began attending church with the family, got baptized as a way to show her commitment to Jason, and spent her weekends volunteering at a Christian youth camp. All these behaviors created a détente between her and Jason's mother—until he proposed. When they announced their engagement, his mother pulled Clarissa aside and said it was time for Jason to "get her out of his system and find a real wife."

Jason believed that if Clarissa just continued with her conversion, his parents would eventually come around—without his ever confronting them about their hurtful beliefs and behavior. Clarissa, on the other hand, now wanted to demand that they move far away and cut all ties.

Initially, their triangle looked like this:

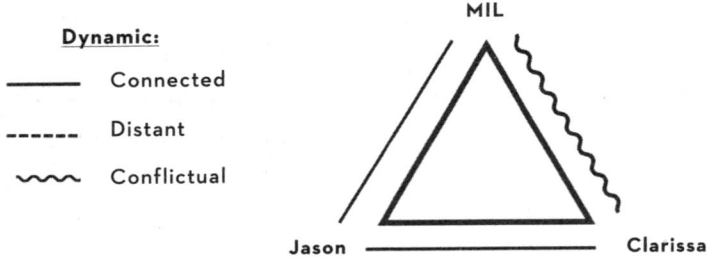

There is tension between Clarissa and her MIL, while there is a positive relationship between mother and son.

Jason, still searching for a middle ground, insisted they get married at his family's church—and invite his family. But four weeks before their wedding, Jason and Clarissa received his parents' RSVP. They declined to attend. Now Jason became extremely angry at his parents, and their triangle changed to look more like this:

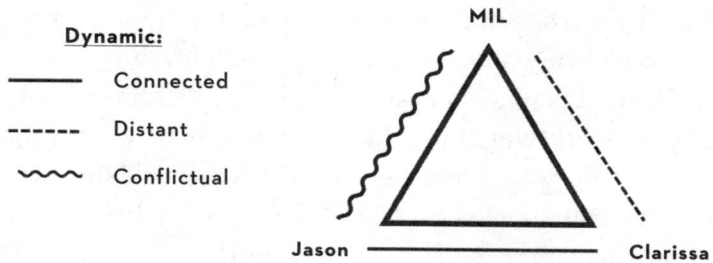

Jason's mother puts pressure on their relationship, which ends up strengthening his bond with Clarissa.

In this triangle, Clarissa's MIL attempted to interfere with the relationship between her son and his partner. She was a Controller MIL who clearly struggled to individuate from her son, unable to recognize that he was allowed to live his own life. Rather than seeing her son as a separate person needing to build his own family, she vilified Clarissa. But the more she made Clarissa out to be a villain, the more conflict she created with her son.

While initially it seemed that Clarissa had "won," she in no way wanted to come between her husband and his family. She was not willing to carry that guilt—or be the target of his resentment in the long run. The triangle still needed to be addressed.

VANESSA AND MARCUS

Vanessa and Marcus, whom we met at the beginning of the chapter, struggled to find healthy boundaries with Marcus's mother, who lived in a different city. When I asked Marcus, he said he had a "good relationship" with his mother and that he'd had a "good childhood." But in our couples therapy, it became evident that he compartmentalized the way his mother acted and the impact this had on him and his wife. He was grateful for what his mother had sacrificed as a single mother to put him through school. However, she had pushed him to go into corporate law, which he ended up hating, and now Vanessa was the primary breadwinner as he transitioned into teaching.

His mother blamed Vanessa for "letting him off the hook" on his legal career, saying things like "What happens when Vanessa has a baby and wants to stop working? Who will support you then? Who will support me? She's made you selfish." Marcus would go silent to avoid a fight, leading his mother to believe that she was right and that Vanessa was the "bad guy." Vanessa wanted Marcus to stand up for her and for their marriage, and when he didn't, this caused conflict between the two of them— but that was easier for Marcus to deal with than confronting his mother would be. In that way, the triangulation alleviated the tension in the relationship between him and his mother.

Vanessa also played a role in the triangle. As a Manager-style DIL, she struggled to set healthy boundaries with her MIL. She grew passive-aggressive toward her MIL, especially when her MIL made derogatory comments in front of her. Instead, she turned to her husband and told him what he needed to be doing. But this only distracted Marcus from the primary conflict between him and his mother.

Here is what their triangle looked like:

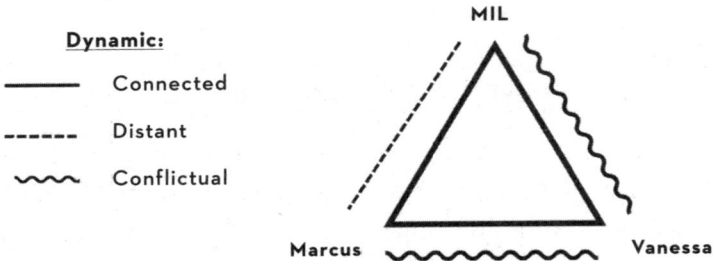

Marcus distances himself from his mother, but this puts pressure on the relationship between his mother and his wife.

Exercise:

Mapping Out Your Triangle

Now that you've read through these stories of triangles, let's work through identifying your triangle. Here are some initial questions to explore what is happening among you, your husband, and his mother. If your partner is open to participating, he can answer these same questions, replacing the word *MIL* with *mother.*

* Can you express separate thoughts and feelings from your MIL? Or do you end up feeling guilty, as if you've done something bad?

* Are you able to tolerate different opinions from your MIL? Or do you try to conform or avoid expressing yourself to your MIL?

* Are you able to recognize when something upsets you and pause before responding? Or do you tend to be more reactive toward your MIL?

* Do you see your MIL as being responsible for her own feelings? Or do you feel overly responsible when she's upset?

* If your MIL is upset, are you able to accept that she's upset? Or do you try to please her or end up creating more distance from her?

* Does your MIL clearly communicate feelings and needs? Or does she push things away, avoid, or communicate in ways that leave people feeling confused and uncertain?

These questions all tap into the level of differentiation and individuation between you, your husband, and his mother. If you noticed that you said yes to the second question in each line (i.e., you tend to take on your MIL's emotions, feel overly responsible for her, and change your own behavior when she is upset), you likely experience more tension and distress when you're in conflict with your MIL.

Now use the questions below to identify the patterns of interaction in your triangle.

* Describe what is happening between you and your MIL when you feel uncomfortable. What does she do? What do you do in response? Are there specific events or topics that lead to certain actions or behaviors?

* Describe what happens between your MIL and your husband. Are there specific events or topics that lead to certain actions or behaviors? What does he do or not do in response to his mother's actions?

* Describe what happens between you and your husband when you feel uncomfortable. What events or topics lead to certain actions or behaviors? What do you do? What does he do? How do you feel together?

* Allow yourself to see your role in the triangle. How do you act and/or react to your MIL and/or husband? Equally important, your husband needs to acknowledge the role that he plays in the triangle. What action, reaction, or lack of action does he take? And what are the consequences?

Spend time exploring where some of the deeper issues might be stemming from for each of you. Do these actions/reactions echo other experiences or relationships? Are there assumptions you, your husband, and/or your MIL are making? While you can't know what your MIL is thinking, you can try shifting your perspective to think about what she might be experiencing that you have not yet considered.

GET OUT OF THE TRIANGLE

Understanding a situation is the first step toward changing it. Now that you understand your triangle, let's explore the steps that you can take to address it.

DIRECT YOUR ANGER AT THE TRIANGLE, NOT THE INDIVIDUAL

It's a protective coping mechanism to project our feelings onto people, especially when we're angry and feel we have been wronged. While your MIL or husband might be doing things that are frustrating or upsetting, it's more productive to focus your anger on the patterns at play, not the people. As a human in my own triangles, trust me when I say this: It feels so much easier to stay angry at the people. I hear you! But it won't change what is happening, and you'll stay stuck in helplessness.

It's important to hold in mind that you and your husband want to be on the same page and find a solution together. Like changing your negative communication cycles by putting you and your partner together against the cycle, you want to see the triangle as something you can both tackle together as a team. This shifts you out of the "you versus me" dynamic and into an "us versus the problem" dynamic. And while I can't speak for your MIL, there are many who are willing to find a different pathway forward once they see that it's less contentious and takes everyone's needs into account.

CONTROL YOUR REACTIVITY

This is a hard step to take because it requires you to practice regulating your emotions in the moment, as they happen. But when you boil over, whether it's with your MIL directly or later on when you're alone with your husband, your reactivity will only leave you further from accomplishing your goals.

When you allow yourself to be reactive and vent to your partner, you might provoke defensiveness in him, leaving him entrenched in the role you don't want him in: siding with his mother against you. You might also step into the overfunctioner role (telling him the problem and the needed solution), which corrals him into the underfunctioner role (being passive and feigning incompetence).

Even as a therapist, I'm not immune to allowing my emotions to boil over. At one family gathering at my in-laws' house, when our son was just five months old, I felt intruded upon by a barrage of commentary on our parenting. Additionally, we had our two-year-old Westie pup, who we were desperately trying to teach not to jump up at the dinner table. Exhausted from losing sleep while away from home and already on guard from the comments coming my way, I saw my father-in-law feeding our dog at the table. In the blink of an eye, I jumped up and snapped, "Don't feed our dog!" Everyone looked stunned, and I felt instantly ashamed as my FIL replied, "I think that's our dog." He was right. Our dogs looked alike.

In retrospect, my outburst was laughable and completely out of character for me. But it spoke to something greater that I was struggling with: How do I respond to these well-intended parenting comments from my in-laws? Bottling it up wasn't working—it only resulted in me exploding. Later, while taking a walk with my FIL and apologizing for my mistake, I told him that as new parents, we were overwhelmed with parenting advice. I expressed appreciation for how much he and my MIL cared for our son, and told him that we just needed to receive more validation and recognition that we were doing a good job. This put an end to the feedback about our parenting choices. But it was also a lesson: I needed to step out of trying to be a good girl all the time and shoving my feelings down until I exploded. I needed to start looking after me.

In order to control your reactivity better, take some time to prepare before entering a situation you predict will be triggering. If you've run yourself ragged cleaning the house and cooking a big meal for everyone, you'll be more likely to behave reactively. If taking a longer period of self-care time before visits with your MIL will help you be less reactive, make that time a priority. Showing up in a less reactive way is more important than having a spotless house.

We tend to act reactively when our thoughts and feelings become overwhelming. This is the fight, flight, freeze, or fawn response we talked about in chapter 6. Yes, you can notice and honor the thoughts and feelings you're having, but you don't have to *behave* based on those feelings. You can use any of the techniques discussed in chapter 6 to help regulate your nervous system. You might also plan ahead of time what to do if you start to lose control. One client found it helpful to go to the bathroom anytime her in-laws started talking about politics. While she knew her in-laws were not receptive to any boundaries she set with them, she made the choice to avoid getting involved and heated with her MIL.

Practice letting go of your sense of responsibility for what other people do. Imagine you have a fence around you and decide what you let in and out. Instead of leaving your gate wide open with your MIL, close it. If your MIL lobs something at you that feels hurtful, you might ask yourself, "What do I want to do with this piece of information? How does it affect me in the bigger picture? Is this something true, or is it just a ball hitting my fence with no consequence to me?" Let the balls she throws bounce off the gate and back at her.

This is also where the practice of individuation and differentiation we talked about in chapter 5 can come into play. Differentiation says, "You and I see this differently, and that is okay."

Individuation says, "These are my thoughts, and I'm still good enough." Put together, they can help you acknowledge that other people might have different ways of thinking about the world without feeling any threat to your sense of self.

Your reactivity can also be managed by building compassion—not just for yourself but also for your husband and your MIL. Self-compassion, as compassion researcher Dr. Kristen Kneff writes, recognizes a painful moment without judgment or self-criticism, acknowledges the common humanity of the situation, and offers kindness, a statement, or even a physical gesture, just like you would give to a dear friend.[2] For example, you might tell yourself, "It makes sense to feel upset. You're learning to step out of this dynamic, and you have a right to struggle with this," while placing a hand on your heart. Compassionate statements for others might sound like "He's doing his best" or "She's repeating what she experienced, and that doesn't make it easy." Understand that you all played a role in getting here based on previous experiences. No one is at fault for the histories they bring into today. You didn't yet have the skills and tools to navigate this. Now you can choose differently.

FOCUS ON THE SELF

When we feel anxious and uncertain in a relationship, we can end up reflexively calling on unhelpful coping mechanisms. You might start to overfunction, taking responsibility for other people and becoming the expert problem solver. Or you might start to underfunction, taking a complete step back and needing someone else to tell you what to do. Or your instinct might be to reach outside yourself, looking to your husband or MIL to change. But in order to tackle the triangle, you need to shift your focus inward.

Shifting the focus inward to the self means releasing responsibility for others' choices and actions, getting curious about the stories you tell yourself, identifying whether they are helpful for you, and coming back to your values to decide how you want to act. This focus is for you—not to please a family member or to discover if you're "good" in the eyes of others.

After that night at my in-laws' table, I had to take a hard look at my actions. Instead of feeling helpless at the dinner table and expecting everyone else to follow my unexpressed wishes, I could have said, "We don't feed our dog at the table, so I'll put him in the other room while we eat," before there was a chance for an incident to occur. But I also needed to have compassion for myself at that moment. I was an overwhelmed, underslept first-time mom, and carrying a heavy mental load that Greg and I were struggling to redivide. But change did not come from telling others how they needed to be different. Change was about focusing on what was within my control—how and what I communicated.

A self-focus also reminds you that you and your partner are on the same page. Instead of building a thick wall, you ask yourself what *you* would like to share at this moment or how you would like to respond, knowing that you can open and close your metaphorical gate as needed. A self-focus removes you from pleasing others while also empowering you to decide what you let in and what you choose to share.

BELIEVE EACH OTHER

Research clearly shows how damaging it is to your relationship to be on different pages when it comes to understanding how hurtful your MIL's words and actions might be.[3] If you're hurting, hearing your partner question, downplay, or deny your feelings, needs, and experiences will only make it worse. What you need to hear from him is: "I believe you." Imagine what it would feel like to hear him say that during a hard moment. For me, it lowers my frustration, brings out my softer side, and tells me that we're in this together.

However, your husband is far less likely to do this if you attack your MIL's character, which pushes him into defensiveness.

That's why instead of focusing on your MIL's character ("She's always out to get me," "She's such an evil woman"), it's more productive to focus on behaviors and actions ("She said X, and that hurt me because Y"). Additionally, instead of using labels for her behavior that your husband might not be able to recognize yet ("She's guilt-tripping us again!"), try connecting a fact with your feeling: "I'm feeling tension because we want to do X but your mother is saying Y."

For your husband's part, suggest to him that instead of defending his mother ("She's just trying to help") or dismissing your experience ("You're making too big a deal out of this"), he should try a statement that validates your feelings ("I can see this doesn't feel good for you"). It would also be helpful for him to practice not immediately trying to find solutions but instead being a witness to your feelings and needs ("Tell me what you need to move forward with this, because I can tell you're hurt").

AVOID REENTERING THE TRIANGLE

When we start to make change, no matter how positive, it can be uncomfortable. It's tempting to return to old patterns, even if we don't like those old patterns, because they feel so familiar and predictable. But when conflict arises or the next holiday arrives, it's worth the extra effort to avoid reentering the triangle you've done so much work to step out of.

Vanessa and Marcus had made a lot of progress. Vanessa had stopped criticizing her MIL to her husband, instead focusing her energy on their marital issues while he addressed building his self-worth. But then Vanessa discovered a text exchange between Marcus and his mother in which Marcus complained about Vanessa's choices for their household budget. This is an example of reentering the triangle: Marcus was pulling his mother back into their marital relationship.

Vanessa and Marcus had to revisit their values and aspirations, specifically regarding who they speak to about their marriage. Although Marcus was initially defensive, saying that he had no one else to talk to about marital problems, Vanessa suggested confiding in a friend or seeing a therapist, reminding him that their goal was to have a positive relationship with his mother. Reluctantly, Marcus started seeing a therapist to address his own struggles with communication and learn to assert himself with his mother and Vanessa.

Gradually, if Marcus's mother came to him criticizing Vanessa, he was able to start calling out her behavior. He began to talk to her about the family's history of trauma, and although she wasn't open to acknowledging her role in their dynamic, Marcus was able to start seeing the familial patterns repeating through the generations and to set more boundaries in the relationship with his mother. Although this cycle breaking was initially hard, it helped Marcus understand that he had unwittingly contributed to his mother's negative view of Vanessa. This took time to change, but the cleaner his relationship with his mother became, the less hostility she directed at Vanessa. Eventually, she was able to engage with Marcus and Vanessa as a team.

MOVING PAST THE TRIANGLE

Angela and John, the couple who moved into the house owned by John's parents, had to refocus their energy on their relationship and work on stepping out of their negative cycle. Once they started seeing that they were on the same team, they were able to find new solutions to their problems.

Angela learned to identify when she was getting critical and started speaking about John's family in fact-based statements instead, which helped John learn to stand down from his defensiveness. She also learned to let go of specific ways her MIL would treat her, practicing depersonalization by saying to herself, "This isn't about me." While it wasn't how she wanted to be treated, Angela learned to self soothe in these moments of reactivity.

For his part, John had to discover his deeper feelings of shame related to his vulnerability, and over time he learned that his family's opinions of him were not a reflection of his self-worth or adequacy. I want to note that John never attended individual therapy, despite his deeper struggles with shame. It wasn't "something you do" in his eyes. Angela had to accept that that was his choice. Over time, though, John began to set boundaries with his mother. He wasn't shutting her out but rather creating healthy distance from her and putting his energy toward his marriage.

While the deed of the house remained under John's family's name, Angela and John began to feel more comfortable making decisions as a family, which often meant not informing his parents about every shelf they hung on the wall. Together, they agreed that it was *their* marital home.

When we get stuck in a triangle, we weaken our relationships and stop being able to meet each other's needs. The next two steps of the VAULT method are going to help you set boundaries and assert yourself—all part of creating a healthy partnership with your husband and finding a way to build a relationship with your MIL. Let's now move into understanding your limits and boundaries.

Chapter 8

LIMITS AND BOUNDARIES

After Values, Aspirations, and Understanding Your Triangle, the next step in the VAULT method is Limits and Boundaries. But despite the ubiquity of the word *boundary* in modern discourse, many people don't truly understand what healthy limits and boundaries are.

On a recent afternoon, I was sitting with two of my closest friends, Rachel and Sarah, sharing small plates at one of our favorite local restaurants. As our roasted cauliflower arrived, Sarah was lamenting her most recent MIL drama. Exasperated, she said, "I just want to draw a hard boundary with my MIL. She needs to change how she's treating me and be willing to apologize for what she's done in the past."

"Well, that's not really a boundary," I said gently, knowing that she was in the same place as so many of my clients when it comes to this topic.

"It's not?" she asked.

"No," I said. "It's a request. And making requests of people often doesn't work if we don't follow up with action."

This is a common misperception, which is why in this chapter, we're going to explore what boundaries actually are, the three requirements for you and your husband to get on the same page about boundaries, and the most common boundary-setting challenges.

WHAT IS A BOUNDARY?

With the increased popularity of the word *boundary*, more and more people come to my office ready to discuss boundaries—but they're often not completely clear on what a boundary is or how to set one. When you make a statement like "I don't want your mother to make comments about my body" or "Please don't talk about our sleeping or feeding decisions for our child," you may think you're communicating your boundaries, but actually you're making a request.

Requests are things that you ask of other people, such as "Please don't come over unannounced" or "I don't want you to bring up politics when we're at the table." Making a request is not a bad thing, but you have to recognize that others may or may not comply with it, because their actions are up to them. Boundaries, on the other hand, communicate what *you* are willing or unwilling to do, such as "If you come over unannounced, I won't answer the door" or "I will not discuss politics at the table."

In her book *Set Boundaries, Find Peace*, therapist Nedra Glover Tawwab states that boundaries require both communication *and* action.[1] This is the key difference between requests and boundaries. You do need to communicate your boundary, but the work doesn't stop there; you also need a plan for what you're going to do to uphold it. If your MIL gives a piece of candy to your child when you've asked her not to, who is stepping in and taking the candy away? If you've expressed to your MIL that you don't want unsolicited parenting advice, how will you change the topic when she starts to talk about sleep training? Preparing yourself to handle these moments is an essential part of boundary setting.

Another common misconception is that boundaries are about creating separation or cutting ties with family. On the contrary, boundaries are pivotal for the health of any relationship. They exist to help foster connection, not division, even if your MIL or other family member might experience them as a separation. When each person in a relationship sets limits and expresses their needs, they're ensuring that resentment is not building in the long run on either side. When you don't set boundaries, you actually run the risk of creating *more* distance between you and the people you love.

You've heard the saying that good fences make good neighbors. That's how I like to think of boundaries. Everything on my side of the fence is my responsibility, and everything on your side of the fence is outside of my control. This is why clearly communicated and consistently upheld boundaries are such a great tool; they're not about trying to control each other's behavior but about taking responsibility for our own.

This also means you can't determine others' boundaries for them, as much as you might want to make your husband start setting limits with his mother. This is what makes it so essential for you and your partner to communicate about values, aspirations, and your triangle in the first three steps of the VAULT method. Once you're on the same team about those things, it will be easier for both you and your husband to start setting boundaries that are beneficial for everyone involved.

This is a lesson I learned the hard way. In my first book, *I Didn't Sign Up for This*, I chose to include some of my own marital struggles with my husband, Greg, especially the challenges we faced once we became parents. Experts are often thought of as being immune to relationship problems, but I like to remind people that everyone struggles with these issues, even professional therapists. Before sharing details of our marriage in such a public way, I asked Greg to read the manuscript and give me his feedback.

One night, after reading through my account of one of our tough marital moments, he said, "I wish I had known then what I know now." This led to a discussion about how he hadn't understood what boundaries were. When I used the word *boundary*, he had only heard me telling him what to do. Basically, he received it as a black-or-white ultimatum, even though that was not at all my intention. He also shared that hearing me say, "You need to set a boundary with your mom," didn't get him any closer to setting a boundary because he didn't really understand what action I wanted him to take. Oof! This was great feedback for me, because on my end, I'd often viewed him as completely unwilling to make any changes. In reality, some of his unwillingness was simply that he didn't know what a boundary was, and he interpreted it to mean something much different from what I meant. In retrospect, we could see the damage this misunderstanding had done to our marital bond.

The difference in our understanding of boundaries was probably especially lopsided because I'm a psychologist, but this disconnect is common between wives and husbands. Women are more likely to consume online content about boundaries, gaslighting, and other psychological terms, while men tend to have less experience thinking and talking about relationship issues. Research on attachment styles also indicates that men are more likely to be avoidantly attached, meaning they're likely to push down their feelings as a coping mechanism and avoid hard conversations rather than learning to talk through conflicts. On top of that, your husband probably has a higher tolerance for the dynamic with his mother because he's more accustomed to it than you are. All of this means that boundary setting might feel extra challenging for your husband—but it's imperative for both partners to learn this skill, as one individual can't solve the problem alone.

Your boundaries will be crossed at some point. Everyone inevitably crosses other people's boundaries sometimes, and that's okay. But that's why it's so important to understand and practice setting healthy limits. This is one way different people coming together learn how to coexist with each other.

THE THREE REQUIREMENTS FOR BOUNDARIES

There are three necessary components to the process of setting boundaries as a solid team: importance, willingness, and ability. When you and your partner both embody these requirements, you reach what I call unity, a place of alignment between you and your partner, where you're on the same team and taking action to implement your shared values and needs by setting limits and boundaries with your MIL. If you lack one or more of these three ingredients, you will likely continue to struggle to make changes as a united front.

Roberto and Estela sat apart from each other on the couch in my office, looking in opposite directions. They had come to me in a deadlock about dealing with his mother when she was visiting from her home country. These visits lasted several weeks at a time, and the last one hit an all-time low for Estela, who had just had their second child.

In our sessions, Estela shared how depleted she was by having to spend the early days of her maternity leave with Roberto's mother: "She critiqued everything I did and was always complaining about something. She did absolutely nothing to contribute to the house and expected to be hosted, even though I was healing from giving birth. And she ate the food that our friends and neighbors made for me to eat in the middle of the night while nursing or when I didn't have energy to make dinner. She kept eating it even after I left notes on the containers."

I could see Estela had lost her sense of power and freedom in her own home. And worse, her husband's approach was leading her to feel even more disrespected.

"My mom doesn't mean to upset you, Estela. It's not a big deal. We can just make more food," Roberto said.

But this only enraged Estela more, especially since it wasn't Roberto making the food. "Your mother should know not to eat my food. I needed you to say something to her, and instead, you sat beside her and said nothing," she said.

As I listened to Roberto and Estela, I could see that they were missing the necessary ingredients for setting successful boundaries. Roberto didn't see the *importance* of boundaries in this situation and therefore didn't have the *willingness* to set them. Estela saw the importance and was willing to set them, but she didn't have the *ability*; she was making requests without follow-up action and then getting frustrated that those requests weren't honored. Over the next several pages, we'll dig into how couples like this can get on the same page about willingness, importance, and ability, thus achieving a sense of unity that lets them successfully set boundaries.

WILLINGNESS

For a couple to set boundaries as a team, they need to have willingness—willingness to get uncomfortable setting boundaries that stem from values and needs, willingness to see the other person's experience. In your relationship, your husband might be completely unwilling to understand what a boundary is or why it's even necessary, saying things like "This is just who she is, so setting a boundary won't matter" or "We have to accept her as she is."

Willingness does accept who people are, but not in a way that avoids dealing with it. Rather, it leans into sitting with your needs, the needs of your partner, the pain of your MIL not being who you wanted her to be, and the possible upset feelings she will have as a response to your boundaries, all of which are generally uncomfortable. A key piece of willingness is accepting that discomfort will be inherent in this process and isn't something that you or your husband should try to overcome, lessen, or avoid. You can trust that the discomfort will reach a peak, as all emotions do, and then fade over time, similar to how an ocean wave rises, crests, and fades away. The goal is to ride the wave of discomfort every time it rises.

Willingness is about being ready to take the steps to make a change. Often, you or your partner might be stuck denying that there's a problem or recognizing that there's a problem but not yet wanting to put in the hard work of changing it. With willingness, you experience a mental shift from "I don't think this is a problem" to "This is something I'm going to do differently." It's a necessary aspect of the ongoing work it takes to set and maintain consistent boundaries, continuously tapping back into your values and needs along the way.

You and your partner will likely experience different levels of willingness depending on the issue, the action required to set the boundary, and the possible implications of the boundary. One or both of you might experience a greater sense of willingness if a boundary feels low-stakes (e.g., turning down a short visit, expressing a food preference) and a lower sense of willingness if a boundary has the possibility to upset the status quo, create difficult feelings for your MIL, or change a dynamic (e.g., addressing unwelcome parenting advice, making decisions that do not include your MIL). As with Roberto and Estela, there is often a mismatch between partners; one is willing to set a boundary, and the other is not. Let's talk about what each partner can do if that's the case.

For the Willing Partner

In some ways, it's easier to be the willing partner. You know what you want and see the pathway forward. You're ready to get uncomfortable. You know what needs to change. I also appreciate, however, that in this position you might feel a complete loss of power because you have to wait for your partner to be willing as well.

When we lose our sense of power, we often get frustrated and start doing things that backfire and keep us stuck longer. In many of my therapy sessions, I've seen the willing person push their partner to start making change *now*, but this pushing just leads their partner to dig their heels in more. This can sound like one partner saying, "You need to set this boundary with your mother," while the other person says, "I don't see the issue here." It's normal and common for both people to argue over who is right or wrong, but these conversations tend to result in dead-end debates that don't help you move through the conversation any faster or bring your partner any closer to willingness.

How you approach your partner's level of willingness is important to consider. I like to use strategies from an approach called *motivational interviewing* with clients who struggle to change.[2] Instead of trying to convince them to change, you first need to be able to hear your partner's struggle and then be willing to ask questions that bring about change (which I provide below).

When you first make space for your partner's feelings, you aren't saying that they're "right" but rather indicating that all feelings are okay. Instead of telling yourself that validating your partner's fear of discomfort disqualifies your feelings, remind yourself that two truths can coexist simultaneously. You can refrain from taking responsibility for your partner's feelings while also maintaining emotional closeness to him. This is particularly challenging in a relationship but also can bring great rewards when hard choices are made.

You'll then want to start asking questions that help create a desire to change. Here are some questions you can ask your partner to help increase their willingness to make a shift. Remember that when asking these questions, you want to remain in a position of being open and understanding. Turn up the curiosity. This likely won't be a one-time conversation but rather a series of discussions related to when change can actually happen.

* How would you like things to be different?

* What do you hope this situation could look like with your mother?

* What do you think needs to happen around this situation?

* What do you know about yourself that will help you set this boundary?

* What areas are you willing to change?

* What's the downside of how things are going right now?

* What are the potential benefits of setting the boundary? What are the potential costs of setting the boundary?

* What are the potential benefits and costs of *not* setting the boundary?

* If we think of where we want to be as a couple in five years, what do we want to be able to say about this time when it comes to dealing with your mother?

The questions above are open-ended questions, which help stimulate talk related to change. Notice that in these questions, you're not asking, "Why?" Questions like "Why won't you change?" or "Why can't you see it my way?" lead people to dig in their heels and become firmer in their beliefs and opinions. Don't ask, "Why do you have to keep doing this with your mother?" or "Why can't you just do what we talked about?" Instead, focus forward on change and what your potential future could look like if you approach this issue differently.

For the Unwilling Partner

When one partner says, "You need to set a boundary!," it usually doesn't make the other partner more willing to do so. The unwilling partner will likely become defensive and, like my husband, may not even fully understand what is being asked of them. When there is a struggle with willingness, it's important for you and your husband to sit down and talk about your intentions in creating a boundary and what that boundary would actually look like. Here are some questions to help the unwilling partner explore their feelings:

* What happens if we stay the same?

* What thoughts and fears do I have around setting this boundary?

* What would it be like to make space for change?

* Would I be willing to change in order to disrupt these hurt feelings my partner is experiencing?

* What is being asked of me, and can I try it out for a period of time?

* What do I like or dislike about my mother's or parents' behavior that I don't want to keep repeating?

* If our children were in this position, what would I want them to experience?

* What could be the benefits of trying this as an experiment to see what happens?

Often, a partner isn't fully unwilling but merely ambivalent; they're not sure whether they want to make a change or not. This is not necessarily a bad thing. While Roberto started from a place of ambivalence, he began seeing that, while it wasn't helpful for Estela to keep telling him what to do, he did need to explore his own sense of willingness, the costs of continuing to downplay his wife's feelings and placate his mother, and what he might gain from being uncomfortable with his family of origin.

Although he didn't yet have the skills to assert his and his family's needs, through our work together, he moved into taking action, seeing that he wanted to feel better in his marriage.

IMPORTANCE

Importance is about understanding why certain limits and boundaries are essential for you, your relationship as a couple, and also your relationship in the triangle with your mother-in-law. When we recognize the importance of a boundary, we are saying to each other, "I see that this matters to you, and so it matters to me too." This builds a sense of emotional security and connectedness. It is a continuation of the first two steps of the VAULT method, Values and Aspirations. You are on the same team, you share your values, and you appreciate that you are *both* putting your relationship first. *My boundary* then becomes *our boundary* as you walk in this space together.

When it comes to expressing the importance of a boundary, we often get stuck in reactivity. You might find yourself saying something unspecific like "This is my boundary," "I don't need to explain this," or "This is just what I need." This is sure to backfire with your partner, because they will fail to grasp the importance of your boundary. In an interdependent romantic partnership, it isn't sufficient to say, "This is my boundary." That doesn't facilitate connection, closeness, or emotional safety.

You can determine and communicate the importance of a boundary by identifying the core needs underlying it. The identification, expression, and owning of your needs allows you to have a sense of true connection with yourself and with others. Note that needs are not the same as expectations, even though we often express expectations in the form of a statement like "I need you to say no to your mother" or "I need your family to stop swearing in front of our kids." As we discussed in chapter 4, core needs are about our fundamental psychological, emotional, and physical well-being, whereas expectations are beliefs and assumptions about how a situation "should" be. Expectations are actually flexible and can be negotiated, and treating them as though they're core needs can lead to more defensiveness and less understanding from your partner.

This is part of why Roberto couldn't understand Estela's experience. When Estela said, "I need your mom to stop eating my food," he thought her need was to have food ready to eat when she wanted it. Setting a boundary with his mom didn't seem that important to him when he could find another solution to the problem, like making more food. In Roberto's eyes, this was the path of least resistance, creating less tension with his mother during her stay. In actuality, Estela's need was for something much deeper—a sense of safety and agency in her own home. When Roberto understood her need in those terms, it was easier for him to see the importance of the boundary. He saw that her core need outweighed his desire to simply take the easy road. We all understand each other's boundaries better when they don't seem arbitrary but instead are connected to our values and core needs.

Exercise:
Identifying the Need Behind a Boundary

This exercise will help you understand the core need underlying the boundary you want to set. Answer the following questions in order.

1. What is the problem I am currently having?

2. What thoughts and feelings am I having about this problem?

3. What is this problem really about for me?

4. What thoughts do I have *about myself* now that this is happening?

5. What do I feel *about myself* now that this is happening?

6. And when I think and feel this, what does it mean *about me*?

7. Continue to ask yourself, "What does this mean about me?" until you arrive at a statement that starts with "It means I am . . ." For example, "It means I am not seen and understood by my partner" or "It means I am not worthy of being listened to." This is a core belief that you have about yourself.

8. Now take that "I am" statement (your core belief) and challenge it by saying to yourself, "This belief is just a belief and does not define me. When I get stuck in this belief, what do I need to help me feel loved, worthy, and enough? I need . . ." End the sentence with one of the eight core relational needs: safety, love and belonging, attention, validation and recognition, connection and intimacy, power and agency, freedom and autonomy, or play and fun (see pages 79–83 for more details on each).

9. Finally, take that "I need" statement and use the list of core needs below to complete the following sentence with the corresponding phrase. "This boundary is important to me because I need . . ."

   * **Safety:** ". . . I need to feel emotionally safe, to be respected, to be vulnerable and seen by you."

   * **Love and Belonging:** ". . . I need to know that I matter and belong."

   * **Attention:** ". . . I need your physical presence and attunement."

* **Validation and Recognition:** ". . . I need to know that you see all that I do and how I contribute to our relationship."

* **Connection and Intimacy:** ". . . I need to have quality time together and feel a sense of closeness."

* **Power and Agency:** ". . . I need to have a sense of choice and control."

* **Freedom and Autonomy:** ". . . I need to feel that I can nurture my own independence and identity."

* **Play and Fun:** ". . . I need to experience laughter and lightness together."

When we consider the importance of boundaries as a team, it's important to remember that different issues may seem more or less important to different people. One partner may consider something to be a 10 out of 10 on the importance scale, while the other may see it as a 6. In an interdependent relationship, we co-construct importance, recognizing that what matters to you also matters to me. Here are some questions to help you see eye to eye on the importance behind the boundary:

* What is truly important about setting this boundary?

* On a scale of 1 to 10, 1 being not important at all and 10 being very important, how important is this boundary?

* What are the steps I can take toward this boundary?

* What could I/we gain from setting this boundary?

* If we're putting our relationship as the top priority, what would I need to consider to ensure that we're on the same team?

* Can I identify the thoughts and feelings that stop me from seeing what truly matters here? What can I do to unhook myself from those thoughts and feelings, acknowledging that thoughts and feelings are not truths?

* What are a few things that I have avoided in my life because of anxiety, uncertainty, or fear? What benefits might I experience by doing something that matters to me, even though it makes me feel anxious or scared?

In therapy, I helped Estela talk about her feelings of not being seen and chosen by her husband. When I asked about what or who her MIL's criticisms reminded her of, she recalled a history of emotionally abusive comments from her mother that made her feel like she was a problem and an inconvenience to the whole family. Roberto had never connected Estela's distress to her upbringing, despite knowing that Estela's mother was toxic. He began to better understand the importance of her need for boundaries.

Meanwhile, when we explored what was important for Roberto, he shared that he didn't want ongoing conflict with his wife and his mother. Recognizing that he couldn't change either woman, I asked him to consider what this was about for him: If his wife and mother were happy, what would it mean *about him*? His answer was a window into his needs: He said it would mean that he was a good husband and son, that he was enough. Once Estela saw Roberto's resistance to setting boundaries as part of his fear that he wasn't enough for his wife or his family, she understood where he was coming from. Together, the couple could then see that doing something different was important to both of them.

ABILITY

Once you've recognized the importance of a boundary and become willing to set it, the last element you need is the ability to set it. This is about having the skills to know how and when to communicate a boundary and to understand its constraints. If you're not sure where to start, don't worry, we'll get into precisely *how* to set a boundary a little later in this chapter.

For now, I want to say that, as with any skill, setting boundaries will feel uncomfortable at first, but with practice and time, you'll gain confidence. You probably won't get it right the first time, and you'll make mistakes along the way. Allow each other the space to fumble, and allow yourself to be open to learning what you could do differently next time. This requires both partners to have compassion for each other along this journey. Here are a few questions you can ask to tap into your sense of confidence about your ability to set a boundary:

* What traits do you know about yourself that will allow you to set a boundary?

* How confident are you that you could set this boundary with your mother/MIL?

* If you were actually to set a boundary with your mother/MIL, how could you do it?

* How confident are you that you could communicate this to your mother/MIL? Very confident or not at all confident?

Like many of us, Roberto and Estela had both grown up in families where boundaries were not modeled to them, and no one had ever taught them how to clearly and concisely communicate their needs and limits in a way that allows the other person to understand them. While Estela had already built separation and individuation with her mother by setting firm limits around spending time with her, that didn't mean she automatically knew how to set boundaries with a different person in a different situation. Roberto had even less experience with the ins and outs of boundary setting, so it was an even bigger learning curve for him. Both partners had to work on their ability to communicate and uphold limits with awareness, intentionality, and compassion. We'll tackle the how-to throughout the remainder of this chapter.

SETTING BOUNDARIES
WITHOUT UNITY

With the combination of willingness, importance, and ability, you and your partner can achieve the unity necessary to set boundaries as a team. But what if you're there and your partner isn't? If your husband is not able to do this work yet, it will be time to practice acceptance toward your husband and the situation. You cannot change others, but you can ask yourself how you would like to continue to show up, acknowledging without judgment that this is where your partner is right now. You can accept both the reality of your husband's behavior and your anger that he is not ready to change.

However, I want you to hear me on this: Your husband can't ask you to "just be happy" if he isn't willing to share your needs as a couple. He, too, will need to sit with his discomfort and accept that you're in a different place than him. This doesn't give you permission to rage at him or treat him badly, but I do want you to know that your feelings are valid. It hurts not to have your partner do this with you. When we practice differentiation, we see that both experiences are true: He is not ready to make changes, and you are not happy about this. When couples reach this impasse, I think of the quote from economist Thomas Sowell: "There are no solutions, there are only trade-offs."

What this means for you is that you will need to create self-boundaries, that is, commitments to yourself to protect your peace and make choices in your best interest. These are not ways to retaliate or make a passive-aggressive statement to your husband. They are limits you set to protect your overall emotional and mental well-being. You matter too. Here is a list of some self-boundaries you might find useful to consider.

* Choose not to open a text message.

* Decide to stay home when your husband goes to his parents' place.

* Change the topic of conversation when it no longer feels good.

* Refrain from overexplaining your need or decision.

* Step away from disagreements before they become heated.

* Change a previous agreement because you no longer feel good about it.

* Silence a phone call when you're not in the right headspace to take it.

* Decide to stay quiet in a conversation that you no longer want to engage in.

* Ask for help, even when it feels hard.

* Don't apologize for things that are not your fault.

* Prioritize your own mental health and wellness.

* Allow others to make mistakes and don't expect perfection from them (or yourself).

POROUS, RIGID, AND HEALTHY BOUNDARIES

It wasn't until after the birth of my second child, several years into my career, that I realized with a shock that I had major boundary problems. Although I teach people about boundaries every day, I would agree to meet my friend and her baby at ten o'clock when I really needed it to be two, or to travel long distances to family events despite having the youngest kids of anyone involved. I was caring for everyone but myself, only to find myself resenting the people closest to me because I wasn't expressing what I needed. This is a great reminder that even when we know a lot about boundaries, we don't always get them right. We aim for boundaries with a healthy level of flexibility, but sometimes we end up making them overly porous or overly rigid.

Porous boundaries are those that are too easy for others to cross. Perhaps you say you're going to stop loaning money to a family member who never pays you back, but every time they ask, you end up giving in. If you tend to have porous boundaries, you're likely a Good Girl–style daughter-in-law who doubts your self-worth and views pleasing others as a way to maintain a close relationship. You question your values based on who you're with and their needs. Saying no is deeply uncomfortable for you. It's most common for caregivers and women to find themselves with porous boundaries, but men can struggle with them as well, especially with their mothers. There's a cost to being this type of boundary setter: When you're meeting everyone's needs but your own, you can start to feel resentment.

In contrast to porous boundaries, rigid boundaries lack flexibility and are too difficult for others to comply with. You might establish a naptime for your kids and then insist that it happen at exactly the same time every day, even on days when someone else is watching them or the day's normal schedule is altered because of a visit from an out-of-town relative. Once a rigid boundary is set, there's no room for modification. If you tend to have rigid boundaries, you're likely a Manager-style DIL who holds onto perfectionism and high standards as a way to ward off chaos and instability. Asking for help typically feels out of the question. The cost is that you keep others from truly getting close to you and might unintentionally create drama with loved ones who fail to meet your standards. Holding rigid boundaries can end up creating walls instead of bridges and gates.

In the middle is the happy medium: healthy boundaries. This might mean loaning money to a family member once or twice but stopping once it becomes clear they never pay you back, or having a consistent naptime for your kids but being flexible about it during atypical situations. This is about finding equilibrium by tuning into your values and wholeheartedly believing that your needs and wants are valid so that you won't change your mind later because of guilt or defensiveness. (I wish I could say that you simply won't feel guilty or defensive, but emotions are trickier than that.) This takes a lot of work. Flexing to create connection while simultaneously trusting that you don't have to self-sacrifice is a hard skill to master—especially if you feel like you've been taken advantage of or manipulated in previous situations by your MIL or husband. But it's not impossible. In the next section, we'll dive into how to set a boundary in detail.

HOW TO SET A BOUNDARY

At this point, you may be thinking, "Boundaries sound great, but how do I set one?" I love the expression "Hard on the inside, soft on the outside."³ I take this sentiment to mean that, together with your partner, you are firm on the core of what you desire and need, *and* you are kind and empathetic to others as you set boundaries. This section will cover how to set a boundary. Ideally, this is work that you want to do together with your husband, but if he's not on board, you'll still benefit from doing it on your own.

To respectfully and effectively set boundaries, start by empathizing with the other person. Let them know with kindness that you see them and their good intentions. Then assert your needs, clearly and concisely, focus on using "I" statements. If the person you're speaking to (such as your MIL) struggles to see your emotions, consider keeping this part brief. Finally—and this is the most important piece—share how you want to move forward.

Here are some examples.

Example: Your MIL makes a comment on your parenting choices, saying, "This isn't what we did in my day."

Your Boundary: "You contributed so much to your son's upbringing. It's now our turn to be parents. If you feel the need to give advice on parenting, we can set a specific time to do this together one day, and we'll be open to hearing what you have to say."

Shortened Statement: "Our parenting is going to look different, and we're okay with that."

Example: Your MIL gives a significant amount of money to you and your partner.

Your Boundary: "This is a generous gift, and we're grateful for it. It's important to us that this type of gift doesn't come with strings attached. We can accept this gift only if we are free to do what we want with it."

Shortened Statement: "Thank you for this generous gift! We can only accept it if we are free to do what we want with it."

Example: Your MIL pulls your husband and/or you into drama with another family member.

Your Boundary: "This is a really difficult situation, and I can see how upset you are. I would prefer not to hear the details and think this would be better addressed with [family member]."

Shortened Statement: "Oh, this is a tricky one. I think it's best to tackle this with that person and not with me. Have you been following any football this year?"

Your boundary statements might change depending on the context. In an urgent, safety-related situation, you might skip all the steps and say, "The baby's car seat buckles need to be tighter," then step in and tighten the buckles yourself. If you're dealing with someone who frequently pushes your boundaries, you might say, "I'm picking up the baby and putting her to sleep now" without further explanation or justification.

Many people get stuck in overjustifying and overexplaining their boundary. This is what would happen for Helena from chapter 1, who tried over and over again to explain co-sleeping with her child to her MIL. When she finally responded to her MIL's questions with "I know how much you love our child. I am not willing to talk about our sleep choices with you," she could see the look of surprise on her MIL's face. But she successfully moved on to a new topic of conversation, and co-sleeping never came up again.

One of the best ways you and your husband can learn to express your boundaries is by writing them out in advance. Sit down together and have a few options ready, using the words that feel right for you. Remember that you might also choose to modify your boundary statement. For example, if your Controller MIL continues to bring multiple gifts for the children even though you've asked her not to, you might choose to simply thank her and donate them afterward. If your Blamer MIL targets you with another critical statement, your silence might be how you state your boundary that you are no longer engaging in this conversation. Complete your plan by agreeing on the action you'll take if your boundaries aren't respected. Here are some examples:

SITUATION	BOUNDARY	ACTION
Your future MIL tells you who should be invited to your wedding.	State that you're doing your best to consider everyone's needs, and you will be the ones to choose who attends your wedding.	Do not discuss wedding details with your future MIL.
You asked your MIL not to come over unannounced, but she shows up for tea.	Restate that you need notice before she comes over to visit.	Set a plan for communicating when she can come over and not letting her in when she arrives unannounced.
Your MIL calls your husband to complain about his sibling (another triangle!).	Express empathy for your MIL's difficult experience and state that it's best to speak to the sibling about the issues they're having.	Change the topic. If necessary, end the phone call when she starts to talk about the sibling.
Your MIL starts to complain about her recent illness, which is a common way she guilts you and your husband.	Validate her pain and state that this is a conversation she needs to have with her physician, therapist, sibling, or a friend.	Avoid asking follow-up questions. Change the topic, end the phone call, or leave the table.
Your MIL says that if you don't spend Christmas with her, she'll be all alone.	Express empathy for her feelings and state that you look forward to the time you will have when you get to connect.	Maintain your plans for the holiday season so that you don't burn out.

COMMON BOUNDARY QUESTIONS

Most conversations about boundaries with clients, friends, and other family members lead to questions such as:

* Is my boundary okay?

* Is this an acceptable need and limit?

* Am I being mean?

* Is it okay for me to want this?

When we ask if our boundaries are okay, I believe we are really asking, "Am I a good person?" To be a healthy boundary setter, you need to start from the place of trusting that you are inherently worthy and that boundaries are not attached to your lovability. You are allowed to say no and still be a good person. (Repeat that as many times as necessary.)

That said, there are certain factors you and your partner can consider to make sure you're coming up with the most productive boundary you can, one that represents your values and needs as a couple and is neither overly porous nor overly rigid. Try asking yourself the following questions.

How would I like to receive this kind of information? Leaning into empathy and compassion is one of the best ways to lower the other person's defensiveness and foster openness to what you have to say. Even if you don't think the person you're setting the boundary with is capable of understanding your experience, ask yourself what a reasonable person would want to hear or how you would share this with a respected colleague or dear friend. I know it can feel vulnerable, but you might get a better response.

What kind of relationship do I currently have with the person I'm setting a boundary with? Be honest with yourself and your partner about this relationship. Is it a deep, emotionally connected bond? Or is it one-sided? Does the parent take time to genuinely hear and understand the adult child's feelings and needs? Are these the kinds of conversations that you have in this family? Some people respond well to a detailed explanation or expression of emotion. With others, a boundary needs to be set with actions.

Will explaining the boundary help? If you aspire to a mutually respectful relationship with your MIL, consider giving her more details to help her understand where your boundary is coming from. There has been a huge generational shift in lifestyle and parenting choices, and your MIL genuinely might not understand your reasoning unless you explain it to her. One man I worked with shared with his mother, "This is how things work today. I'm just as much a primary caregiver as my wife. You need to come to me with these things, not to her." Then again, explaining might not help. A healthy boundary setter prepares themselves by acknowledging other people might be upset about their boundaries. This does not make your boundary wrong, and it does not make you bad. It means that you're creating a relationship that works for both of you without building resentment or walls.

What type of person am I communicating with, and what is the context of the situation? In high-emotion moments with family (e.g., you and your MIL get into an argument at your child's birthday party), you might choose not to address the bigger issue at that time. Once emotions are calmer and you've had a chance to reflect on what happened, ask yourself, "Can she hear my feedback on what happened? Or is she a type of MIL that can't make space for me having a different experience from her? Is this a person with lower emotional and social awareness?" If your MIL has shown that she can learn from her mistakes, sometimes it's best to give grace. Conversely, sometimes it's best to let go of a situation because we know addressing it will not move the needle, and conflict will only end up continuing; this is also one of the ways you can step out of the triangle.

And finally: *Who should communicate the boundary?* This is the second most common question I get around setting boundaries with your MIL, after "Is my boundary okay?" Whether you or your husband should be the person to set and uphold a given limit will vary depending on who you both are, who your MIL is, and the nature of your triangle.

Jamila, whom you met in chapter 1, had a healthy relationship with her Supporter MIL, and felt comfortable setting limits with her. She described giving feedback to her MIL about not buying more toys as holiday gifts for the kids, which her MIL respected. However, there were times around difficult topics (e.g., when her father-in-law was in the hospital) that Jamila requested that her husband take over communication.

When there is persistent conflict or difficult dynamics with your MIL, it's usually better for your husband to communicate boundaries to her (though that's not a hard rule, as there might be scenarios where you step in to assert your needs). If setting a boundary with your MIL has made you the "scapegoat" or "bad guy," your husband will need to work to assert your family needs as a united front: "This is what works for *our family*," "*We* have decided on this."

UNITY AND BOUNDARIES

As spring returned and it was time for Roberto's mother to arrive for her annual stay, the couple was now armed with the knowledge that Estela needed safety and connection with Roberto, and Roberto needed to maintain connection with both his wife and his mother. I encouraged them to write out the top one or two boundaries that they were going to work on in building a healthy relationship with the MIL.

Together, they agreed that, once a week, they would head out on an outing without his mother. This helped meet both Estela's need for connection with Roberto and Roberto's desire to have his mother connected with him and their children during the week. With Roberto's support, Estela began expressing boundaries to her MIL. When her MIL made comments about her parenting, she told her MIL that her comments were not helpful. When her MIL criticized her housekeeping, Estela ignored it and continued living in her home the way she wanted to. While she was never able to change the barrage of negativity, Estela came up with an analogy to help her build self-boundaries: She would practice "being a lamp" and choose what she wanted to shine a light on. In this case, it would be her husband and children. She didn't have to waste her glow on a woman who wasn't interested in building a positive relationship. It wasn't a realistic option not to have her MIL stay with them, but Estela still found a way to reprioritize herself and her marriage.

When couples build their sense of unity around limits and boundaries, they become more successful in upholding their needs while also deepening their connection and their overall sense of emotional safety in the relationship. Now that you have identified your boundaries, you're ready to take action and move toward creating a more meaningful approach to your relationship with your husband and his mother, which we'll do in the fifth and final step of the VAULT method. Let's keep going!

Chapter 9

TAKING ACTION

When Evie was dating Geoff, she loved how close his family was. His parents and his sister's family all lived nearby and were very involved in each other's lives. Geoff was an anesthesiologist, meaning his schedule was unpredictable because surgeries frequently ran long. Working in finance, Evie also had a demanding schedule, but she imagined they'd receive a lot of support from Geoff's close-knit family after they had children.

However, far from stepping in to help with their grandson, who was followed by another boy a couple of years later, Evie's in-laws disapproved of her going back to work after having kids, and they believed that if they stepped in to offer childcare, they were "letting her off the hook" for her choice to work outside the home. Evie was hurt and insulted by this but decided to accept the situation as it was.

This strategy worked reasonably well—until Geoff's sister went through a divorce and his parents stepped in to co-parent with her, driving her three children to all their activities and actively working to reduce her workload. This disparity in treatment hurt Geoff as well as their children, who were aware that

Nana and Pop-Pop attended all their cousins' games and recitals but none of theirs. When Geoff confronted them at Evie's urging, they would say, "You're being selfish. You have everything, and your sister has nothing." This left Geoff feeling like a bad brother—and then he got angry at Evie for pushing him to raise the point. Evie knew Geoff was as hurt by his parents' behavior as she was, but it was easier for him to be angry at Evie than at them.

A typical exchange would involve Evie's mother-in-law bragging about how great her other grandchildren's school event had been while Evie watched Geoff gradually cloud over. When Evie lost the ability to stay calm and said something about it, her MIL would get angry and defensive, and Geoff would turn his hurt into anger at Evie for upsetting his mother.

Evie knew they needed to find a way to navigate family gatherings that stopped this cycle. It was exhausting and unproductive, and it was driving a wedge between her and Geoff, who was hurting as badly as she was. They needed the VAULT method.

In your own journey through the VAULT method, you have reached the final step. You've established your Values and Aspirations, you Understand Your Triangle, and you've learned how to set Limits and Boundaries. You're now ready to Take Action. In this chapter, you'll learn how to turn all your insights into concrete actions to improve your relationship with your MIL—and your spouse.

Before going further, I want to acknowledge the hard truth: Trying to repair this relationship is a heavy load, and your MIL probably isn't helping you carry it. I regularly hear comments like "Why do I have to be the one to do this work?" and "My MIL isn't willing to change, so why should I be?" But I also want you to hear this: You are doing this work for you and your marriage (and your children, if you have them). With that in mind, it's time to move forward with an action plan.

Ready? Let's go!

STAYING IN ALIGNMENT

Taking action is hard, and you'll inevitably hit some roadblocks along the way. So before we get into specifics, I want to offer you a few principles that you and your spouse can return to in order to get back in alignment when things feel hard, different, or uncomfortable. They will help you remain connected and functioning as a team so you can carry out your action plan—together.

CONNECTION OVER PERFECTION

Now that you have access to new tools and knowledge, you may feel pressure to stop making mistakes and start "getting it right" with your mother-in-law from here on out. The truth is that you're human and you're going to make some missteps as you start taking action, especially at first. If you, like me, struggle with perfectionism, I want to remind you that perfectionism doesn't actually help us reach our goals—it is a maladaptive desire to control outcomes so that we can avoid feeling discomfort and uncertainty.

Let me reassure you that as long as you're prioritizing your connection with your partner, you'll start seeing positive changes in how you feel with your mother-in-law, even if you don't always get everything right. If you tend to get stuck in the all-too-familiar black-and-white paradigm, try to find more areas of gray. Not every single event with your MIL needs to be processed deeply, and not every boundary you set will be perfectly calibrated to give you the result you want. Sometimes, you miss it. But that doesn't mean you give up on connection.

DIFFERENT IS NOT BAD

A common complaint women express in my office: "He doesn't do it how I do it." This could be about anything—a household task, a parenting choice, or communication in general. I recognize how natural it is to desire sameness. When you and your partner do something the same way, it offers a sense of validation: "If we agree, then I'm okay." But sameness does not create a true sense of security. On the contrary, emotional safety and connection come from honoring our differences.

So often we turn to our partner and expect them to approach life the same way we do. But our goal in building secure relationships is accessibility and responsiveness. Instead of requiring your partner to do something the same way you do, take in how responsive he is to you and your needs. Maybe he squeezes your hand instead of intervening when his mother tells your kid to "clean your plate," or he says, "Mom, enough," instead of delivering the detailed boundary statement you rehearsed together. Although these actions might not be how you would approach the situation, you can recognize that they indicate your partner is being responsive to you and letting you know that you're on the same team.

GIVE FEEDBACK, NOT DIRECTIVES

When people are told what to do, they often feel their autonomy is being threatened and end up doing the opposite. It's called psychological reactance, and it explains why advice giving and directives tend to backfire. Feedback, in contrast, focuses on helping the other person see the impact of their behavior and creating a collaborative plan to move forward.

To give feedback to your MIL or husband, start by identifying something that they did well. Praise them or express appreciation for their efforts. This recognition goes a long way in helping others lower their defenses and be more open to hearing what you have to say next.

Then express what is happening to you with the formula "fact plus feeling." This lets you focus on a behavior rather than attacking the other person's character. This might sound like saying to your MIL, "When you make comments about my body (fact), I feel upset (feeling)," or saying to your husband, "When you didn't tell your mom that we weren't available for dinner next week (fact), I felt disappointed and confused (feeling)."

After identifying the emotion, talk about the impact their behavior has on you. Talk about the story you tell yourself, what this reminds you of, or the ways this affects your relationship.

Last, once you've given the feedback, you can talk about how you can move forward. What would this involve, and who would be doing what?

Evie, for example, started saying to Geoff before they went to his parents' house, "I love that you keep trying with them, and I respect that this relationship is important to you. When your mother shows a clear preference for her other grandchildren, I feel sad. You don't have to do anything with that information. I just want you to know because you're my partner."

Exercise:
Identifying Strengths

It's easy to get caught in cycles of criticism and defensiveness, pointing out the negative and getting stuck in anger and resentment at what our partner isn't doing. Instead, I want to encourage you to start leaning into the strengths that you each bring to the table, such as empathy, problem-solving, and playfulness, so that they can become part of the solution. You'll each have different strengths, and that's a good thing. A strong team isn't made up of people who have the same skills—it's made up of people with *complementary* skills.

Using the list below, identify what you and your husband are naturally good at when navigating the relationship with your mother-in-law.[1] Place an *I* next to strengths you feel are yours, and an *H* next to strengths you think are your husband's. Incorporate your strengths into your plan for how you move forward.

Adaptable

Ambitious

Articulate

Calm

Candid

Capable

Charismatic

Clearheaded

Communicative

Competitive

Considerate

Cooperative

Courageous

Creative

Curious

Decisive

Dedicated

Determined

Devoted

Diligent

Efficient

Emotionally intelligent

Empathetic

Energetic

Enthusiastic

Experienced

Flexible

Focused

Forthright

Frank

Hardworking

Helpful

Honest

Humble

Humorous

Imaginative

Independent

Innovative

Insightful

Intellectually strong

Intuitive

Inventive

Involved

Kind

Mature

Methodical

Meticulous

Motivated

Natural Leader

Neat

Objective

Open-minded

Organized

Outspoken

Painstaking

Passionate

Patient

Perceptive

Persuasive

Polite

Positive

Practical

Proactive

Problem-solving

Prudent

Punctual

Realistic

Reliable

Resourceful

Respectful	Sensible	Thoughtful
Responsible	Sincere	Trustworthy
Responsive	Sociable	Versatile
Seasoned	Systematic	Well-rounded
Self-confident	Team Player/	Willing
Self-directed	Teamwork	
Self-disciplined	Thorough	

Moving forward, integrate these strengths into your action plan. If you tend to be calmer in a storm, you might be the one to take action in a chaotic moment. If your husband is better at saying no to his mother, perhaps all planning and scheduling of family events can run through him. Recognizing your strengths will help you divide responsibilities as a united team, shifting from "Why do I have to do everything?" and "You can't even do this right" to "You and I have these qualities that will help us in these scenarios."

TAKING ACTION: ANTICIPATE

I take a triple-A approach to action: anticipate, act, and adjust. In this section, you'll create a road map based on these three A's. The goal is not to stop your mother-in-law's behaviors (though I know that would be nice) or to do a complete overhaul of what is happening between mother and son (again, I know it would be nice). The goal is to help you and your husband be a united front, collectively creating strength in your relationship with a clear action plan that works for both of you. Creating this plan might also require you to go back and revisit your values (chapter 5) and your aspirations (chapter 6).

The first A in the three A's of taking action is *anticipate*. This means looking ahead at what is likely to happen and creating a plan to handle it. Many couples interact with an MIL without a plan, not sure what to expect. Having assessed your MIL's type, you *do* know what to expect. Of course you can't predict the future, but you can anticipate probable outcomes and be prepared to react productively.

STEP 1

Answer the following questions:

* What is the upcoming event or ongoing issue?

* What are common trends or themes I can anticipate?

* Who typically says what? How do people respond?

* What is the follow-up? What is the fallout?

STEP 2

Write out all the things that happen with your MIL and husband that are difficult to deal with, cause conflict, or create tension, either within yourself, with your kids, or with your husband. Don't filter yourself; this list is for your eyes only.

Once you've generated a list, separate each behavior/action/experience into one of two groups: tolerable behavior and intolerable behavior.

Tolerable behavior is just that: You can tolerate it. These are actions or comments that are uncomfortable, mildly frustrating, or annoying but that do not significantly harm your relationship, your children, or your well-being. You don't like these actions, but you still feel empowered to make choices for the greater good of you, your family, and your values. This isn't about accepting abuse but about keeping in mind that this isn't your mother and you don't have to be her best friend.

Intolerable behavior includes actions or comments that significantly cross your boundaries, create emotional distress, result in harm to the relationship between you and your husband, and/or impact your children. This might include consistent disrespect, manipulation, gaslighting, invasions of privacy, and other attempts to undermine your self-worth or injure your marriage.

STEP 3

Looking at the list of your mother-in-law's actions from step 2, group together issues with a common theme. This will reveal different categories or themes under both tolerable and intolerable behaviors. For example, if you've written down "Criticizes our baby's sleep schedule," "Gives certain foods to our kids against our wishes," and "Compares my parenting unfavorably to hers," you might put these together in a category labeled "Parenting Comments." Creating these categories will help you identify and tackle certain recurring issues with your husband or your MIL. This tends to be more effective than playing whack-a-mole and trying to address each individual remark.

STEP 4

Knowing that it is not possible to target all behavior and situations, look at the list of intolerable behaviors and choose your top issue or an issue you expect to arise at an upcoming event. (You can always come back to address the others as time goes on.) Consider the answers to these questions to help you decide what to do next. Remember, the goal of taking action is not to change your MIL but to build a more tolerable environment.

Answer these questions by yourself:

* Knowing what I know about my MIL, is there a chance she'll be able to understand why this behavior is intolerable? What about my husband?

* What is the worst-case scenario of not addressing this issue?

* Who am I trying to protect? Myself? Our relationship? Our kids?

* If I were to choose the path of letting this go, what else would I need to happen or what boundary would I need in place? (For example, you might be okay with your kids staying with your MIL, but only if another adult is present. Note that letting go doesn't mean accepting abuse; it requires you to have boundaries without directly addressing the issue with your MIL.)

* What expectations am I holding? What would it be like to soften those expectations?

Answer these questions with your husband:

* What is something that your mother does that you don't want to keep repeating?

* What different outcome would you like to experience that is within our control?

* Thinking of your own childhood, is there something you were raised with that you don't want to teach our children or do to each other in our marriage?

* What could we do differently to feel more connected and aligned to our values in these moments with your mother?

* What fears do you have related to trying something different?

* What thoughts do you have when you think of this as an experiment?

STEP 5

One of the most powerful agents for change in a relationship is being able to choose your responses consciously rather than re-acting on autopilot. As you anticipate the behavior you've mapped out in the previous steps, choose one of three responses you want to use: address it, leave it, or put it down. Making this deci-sion ahead of time will let you respond the way you want to in-stead of behaving reactively. Let's take a look at each of the possible responses.

Address It

Addressing it means responding directly to your mother-in-law's behavior. Before the visit or event, sit down with your husband and, holding an open and flexible mindset, clarify with him what you both plan to say and do. As you anticipate setting a bound-ary with your MIL, is it something you'll communicate to her directly or a behavior you'll engage in? Boundaries require ac-tion to uphold; what will you do when your boundaries are crossed? Identify what values you're nurturing and the need(s) behind your boundary. Focus on doing things that allow you to be a united front and feel a sense of mutual responsiveness. For example, you might agree that if your MIL comments on your body, your husband tells his mother in the moment that it's not appropriate to comment on his wife's body. Or, if your MIL gives an unsafe toy to your child, either one of you will remove the toy and state to your MIL why it's not safe. Ask for what you need to help you navigate the event.

If any of your MIL's problematic behavior is directed toward your children, depending on their age, speak to them about their feelings about visiting Grandma. They may or may not have noticed some things that don't feel good to them (e.g., "Grandma makes me hug her when I don't want to"). Remind them that, even though there are other adults around, you are their "sturdy leader," as child psychologist Dr. Becky Kennedy calls parents, and you will support them.[2] If they feel uncomfortable, come up with a plan together, either preparing what they can say to Grandma or offering to respond to Grandma for them in the moment.

In some cases, you and your husband might choose to talk to your MIL *before* the event or visit, getting in front of any potential issues by sharing what your expectations and needs are. This can be particularly helpful when it comes to the birth of a baby, big family gatherings, your MIL looking after your child, or the holidays. Recognizing that each person has expectations, ask what her wishes are—assuming that you're flexible enough to accommodate some of her needs. If you're not, simply express what your expectations and needs are for your time together.

Leave It

Leaving it means consciously choosing not to address your MIL's problematic behavior in the moment because you know it won't be productive. This doesn't mean you're walking away from something difficult but rather that you recognize the behavior isn't going to change and you have the tools and resilience to deal with it.

This was a strategy that Pooja and Nick chose with Nick's mother, who believed in traditional gender roles and frequently told their two daughters what they were and weren't "allowed" to do as girls. This went against Pooja and Nick's parenting values, but after several failed attempts to get his mother to stop, the couple shifted their focus to acknowledging each other in the moment and then doing the repair work with their kids once they got home. Together, they developed a ritual of squeezing each other's shoulders when his mother made these comments. It offered reassurance and togetherness, instead of Pooja feeling that she had to defend their parenting choices on her own.

Leaving it doesn't have to be a permanent strategy. It can be helpful to take a step back and ask yourself, "What's a realistic time frame for making these changes or setting these boundaries?" When our expectations are too high, we are more likely to struggle and build resentment. It might be perfectly reasonable to leave something for now and circle back around to address it at some point in the future when it makes more sense.

Put It Down

Imagine that every time you interact with your MIL or go to a family event, you pick up an oversize bucket of conflicts, irritations, and other issues; you hold it tightly, and the weight of it becomes your problem. With this strategy, you simply put the bucket down. You completely accept what is—discomfort, tension, disliking a certain behavior—and stop engaging with it altogether.

If you choose to put it down, completely let it go. No more bringing it up with your husband. No more trying not to be annoyed when the annoying thing happens. You feel your feelings (e.g., "I'm annoyed and frustrated right now and this doesn't feel good") and make space for them without getting hooked by them (e.g., "I don't have to get sucked into this" and "Not my circus, not my monkeys"). This says, "I'm choosing my own peace."

Putting it down might require you to let your husband know that you're doing just that—not that you're walking away from his family but that you're no longer going to participate in trying to solve their drama, change them, or maintain their relationship with your husband. This is where many women tell me they have stopped "kin-keeping" with their in-laws and have given full responsibility for the tasks of communicating, gift buying, and organizing activities back to their husband.

When my clients reach the point of wanting to put it down,

they often tell me that, with hindsight, they wished they had let some things go earlier. Moving forward, the question then changes to "So what *is* important to address?"

STEP 6

Finally, as part of your pre-action planning, you'll want to reassess the ways you spend time with your in-laws. With your husband, discuss if it would work better to spend time with his family in a different way. If you previously stayed at their house while visiting, perhaps you now find a hotel close by to create some healthy distance. Get-togethers might become more time limited and might also happen in more neutral locations. (I have repeatedly worked with people who have more pleasant interactions with their in-laws when they take place outside either party's house.) If random drop-ins have been a frequent point of tension, perhaps it's time to set the boundary that visits need to be planned ahead of time.

If necessary, you can limit overall contact with your in-laws. Pulling back contact might be communicated verbally (e.g., "We won't be attending Sunday dinners every week") or through actions (e.g., spacing out visits, leaving more time before responding to texts, letting the call go to voicemail). I discourage "ghosting" family members, or cutting off contact without notice, which can ultimately leave both parties more hurt. Taking space doesn't have to be permanent; it could be just for now.

TAKING ACTION:
ACT

Remember, the three A's of taking action are anticipate, act, and adjust. Now that you've anticipated a plan of action, it's time to act, with the goal of interacting respectfully with your mother-in-law. Hopefully, you and your husband have decided what to do together, but if your husband is not onboard, you can continue to move forward in ways that prioritize your marriage. Either way, let's talk about the specific communication and relational tools you can use.

RESPONDING IN THE MOMENT

Although it's not always possible, there are several benefits to addressing your mother-in-law's behavior in the moment rather than later. Responding in the moment increases the chances of your boundary being understood, reduces the likelihood of revisionist history, prevents unmet needs from spilling over later, and allows you to be compassionate and quick ("We don't [want/need/do] that, but let's figure something out for next time!"). It's easier to do this when you and your husband have already decided who will be the one to say something.

ASSERTIVE COMMUNICATION

Use assertive communication as you convey your boundaries and discuss your needs and family aspirations. Assertive communication is neither too passive nor too aggressive; it requires you to hold respect for both yourself and the other person. Respecting your MIL might mean saying things like "I know this is not what you wanted" or "I can appreciate that you see this differently." Respecting yourself means expressing what you need and want clearly so that she can understand.

Let's say your MIL texts you about her son's health instead of him. Passive communication would be: "He's feeling better, thanks for asking." This allows your boundaries to be trampled without expressing what you need. Aggressive communication would be: "Why are you texting me?" This communicates your desire not to be texted but doesn't respect your MIL's feelings or intentions. Passive-aggressive communication, the worst of both worlds, doesn't communicate about the problem directly but still conveys hostility behind a veneer of politeness. It might sound something like: "Is his phone turned off? I can ask him to turn it back on so you can text him." What you want to aim for is assertive communication that states your needs while holding empathy for your MIL: "I know you care about him, and he wants to hear from you. Text him directly."

META-COMMUNICATION

Meta-communication is communication about communication, or talking about *how* you're talking about things. This is a great approach when you feel like the conversation is getting derailed, you're repeating yourself, or you're not being understood. It also helps to enhance understanding and empathy between people. A few questions and statements that shift out of communication and into meta-communication are:

* What is happening between us here?

* When I said that, it sounds like you heard me say something different.

* I notice you're reacting to what I just said.

* Can we talk about how we've been communicating?

* It was not my intention to hurt your feelings with what I just shared, but I can appreciate that it doesn't feel good for you.

Meta-communication is most effective with an open and respectful individual. However, it isn't for every relationship, which is why it's important to understand the type of MIL you have, the type of relationship you want to have with her, and the context of the situation. If your MIL is emotionally immature, insecure, or otherwise unable to engage in meta-communication, you're better off simply continuing to hold your boundary (e.g., "This isn't something I'm willing to continue talking about").

ASK MORE QUESTIONS

By asking questions, you are drawing out someone else's intentions and wishes (and giving yourself more time to decide if what they want will work for you). Consider asking your MIL questions like "What did you hope to make happen by doing that?," "What are your desires moving forward?," or "What did you think would come out of that?" These questions require the other person to reflect on their wishes and think more about what has happened and what they want. This is an effective strategy with people who tend to twist situations around on you, refuse to take responsibility in the relationship, or play the victim.

SHARE LESS AND
DISCLOSE CAUTIOUSLY

Instead of opening up about all aspects of your lives, prune back what you share with your MIL. If parenting conversations have become tense, agree that you will no longer enter these conversations. If you've received rude remarks about your own parents, choose not to go into detail about them. Remember that you get to decide how much and what you share with your MIL. There are no requirements for what the interaction looks like. If she desires a closer relationship, it is up to her to build trust and respect through her actions. It is not your job to meet her desires.

CURATE COMMUNICATION
FOR YOUR MIL

Research shows two types of messages from adult children will trigger a greater sense of threat in their adult parents: offering directives and expressing doubt.[3] Yet these are the two most common ways people attempt to communicate with their mother-in-law. It ends up backfiring and escalating into more conflict because it's a *non-accommodating* communication style.

Accommodation, conversely, considers who you're speaking to with the goal of remaining respectful and connected. This approach doesn't mean abandoning yourself or your boundaries. It means adjusting your speech, vocal patterns, gestures, and words when communicating with your MIL, with the goal of feeling more aligned. No, this does not mean that if your MIL is passive-aggressive, you adjust by being passive-aggressive too. Accommodation builds inclusion and connection, with the ultimate effect of making it easier for your MIL to respect your boundaries.

Different MILs may receive some messages better than others. Here are some suggestions for each MIL type based on what has been successful for my clients.

Internalizers

When communicating with a Martyr who offers help that may not actually be helpful and complains that she's underappreciated and poorly treated, try the following:

* Set clear limits regarding what she does for the family. Clearly separate what you're responsible for from what she's responsible for.

* Remind yourself that she's allowed to have her experience, but you're not responsible for it.

* Validate her feelings but not necessarily her perceptions or beliefs.

* It's not your responsibility to fix things for her, so you can put her struggle back on her by asking, "What do you need right now?" or "What did you expect to happen?" You could

also say things like "This isn't something for me to solve" or "You're allowed to feel that way, but it doesn't mean we have to change what we want."

* Explicitly communicate about expectations (e.g., "We will be out for the night and would like you to look after the kids. You can say no.").

* State a fact, express appreciation for what she did, then speak about next time (e.g., "It's a long drive for you to come here. We're glad you came to visit. If this was too hard for you, we need you to say no next time.").

When communicating with a Victim who believes the world is out to get her and complains about her constant misfortunes:

* Avoid problem-solving mode and ask her to generate her own solution: "How do you envision this working? What are you looking for?"

* Offer empathy, but know your limits.

* Give yourself permission to end the conversation. Have a statement ready to change the topic to something more neutral.

* Let your partner absorb the brunt of the complaints.

* Create distance in your mind by imagining this playing out in a television show rather than involving yourself directly in the drama.

* Redefine what time spent together looks like. Try organizing visits around a specific activity, stay busy, and don't expect deep conversations.

Externalizers

If you're communicating with a Blamer who believes you are the source of all the family's problems, try the following:

* Consider the costs and benefits of having your husband handle communicating with your MIL.

* Present a united front with your husband by using "we" language, ensuring you and he have made agreements together ahead of time.

* Shift your focus from trying to correct her vision of you to trying to be on the same team with your husband.

* Avoid doubling down on getting her to see things your way.

If you're communicating with a Controller who insists her way is best and tries to force you to comply with it:

* Avoid arguing with your MIL about who is right or wrong.

* Practice saying, "It's okay if we do it differently."

* Don't try to change her beliefs or viewpoints.

* Choose ahead of time what you want to discuss with her and what you'll avoid sharing.

* Let go of trying to get recognition or validation, as she may not be able to offer this.

Balancers

If you're communicating with a Distancer who respects your autonomy but doesn't participate much in your life, try the following:

* Vocalize your desire for involvement or connection, but be ready to accept her more distant approach.

* Be direct in communication instead of avoiding hard topics.

* Ask yourself what you want and where you would like to focus your energy. If you prioritize a few requests, she may well be able to meet them.

If you're communicating with a Supporter who is able to compromise and see others' points of view:

* Discuss needs and wishes beforehand with your husband; depending on the relationship, either partner can communicate with your MIL.

* Request help directly when needed (e.g., switch "Feel free to come visit" to "I need help with the kids. Could you come on Saturday at lunchtime?").

* Check in with your expectations of her and her expectations of the situation.

* Accept her for who she is versus who you hoped she would be (e.g., maybe she's a helper around the home and not a hands-on grandmother).

TAKING ACTION:
ADJUST

After anticipating and acting, it's time for the third A of taking action: adjusting. After you prepare and carry out your plan of action, evaluate how things went and adjust the plan for next time. Adjusting your plan is just as important as creating one, but unfortunately, many couples struggle to return to hard moments to review how things went. Without this reflection, though, you forfeit the opportunity to learn and improve the situation for you both. By building a regular practice of reflecting on what happened, you create a ritual of coming back together, whether it's during your weekly meeting (which I encourage all couples to have!) or during another time when you can have ten minutes of uninterrupted conversation. Focus first on what worked and what you both did well before moving on to what didn't work; if the focus is too negative, you won't want to keep having this type of conversation.

Exercise:
In Review

After putting your plans into action with your mother-in-law, ask each other these questions to explore what happened and what you might consider adjusting for next time. If your partner is not doing this with you, you can also answer these questions alone.

* How did you feel going into this situation with your mother/MIL?

* What went well for you? What did we do well together?

* How did you feel taking the action that you planned? If you experienced discomfort afterward, how did you cope with it?

* What happened that you weren't prepared for or found difficult?

* What parts were we on the same team for? Were there moments when we felt like we were not a team?

* Were there moments when you felt not supported?
  Tell me about them.

* If we could rewind the tape and do it again, what would
  you want to do differently?

* How successful do you feel we were at staying aligned
  with our values and aspirations?

* Was what we did effective in working toward what we
  want with your mother/MIL?

* How confident are we in our ability to move forward
  with this plan, or do we need to make adjustments for
  next time?

Depending on your relationship with your MIL, you can also
review events with her, though this will be productive only to the
extent that your MIL is able to take in your words. When planning to revisit something as a way to work through the challenges you're having, be sure to use "I" language, talk about your
experience using facts only (e.g., avoid perceptions like "I feel
like you don't care about us" or broad-stroke statements like "You
don't care about us"), and have a clear understanding of what
you need moving forward.

This is also your time to do repair work with your children,
if you have them. Conflict with an MIL at a family event can affect them too. You can't get ahead of every comment or action
that didn't feel good to your kids, but you get to be a secure base
for them to process what happened. Ask them how they experienced the family event and validate any feelings they have. Your
job is not to convince them to accept behavior they don't like but

instead to prepare them for what they could do next time to feel better. You don't have to explain their grandparents' behavior; your only job is to be a witness for your kids.

WHAT TO DO IF YOUR HUSBAND DIDN'T STICK TO THE PLAN

Sometimes you can spend plenty of time and energy planning out what to do as a team with your husband, and then, when the moment arrives, he doesn't do what you agreed he'd do. As this is a new process for both of you, this doesn't necessarily mean that he isn't willing to change. Mistakes happen under pressure. But if it happens repeatedly, you might need a system or a new strategy.

Consider asking him to commit to a prepared response like "Thank you for letting me know. This is something that my wife and I will consider and get back to you" or "I'll need time to think about this." These responses focus on you and your partner as a team and allow you to create a response later when your husband can think more clearly. (Note: Always prioritize safety, so if in the moment, you need to say, "My toddler cannot eat hard candy yet," and physically remove the candy, do so.)

Practice empathy and compassion for your husband. If there's one thing I've come to appreciate about being a psychologist, a mom, and a wife, it's that my empathy bucket is by default much fuller for my kids and clients than it is for my husband, whom I often expect to "just have it together, already." But if the empathy isn't coming naturally, it's important to cultivate it. If you find your empathy bucket is running particularly low, it might also indicate that you're not looking after some of your own needs, both within yourself and in the relationship. Take this as a cue to start sharing some of your feelings and making space for your own self-care.

Gradually, you will build flexibility and patience, recognizing that relationships are not about getting everything right all the time and that change takes time.

WHAT TO DO IF YOUR HUSBAND
WON'T REVIEW WITH YOU

What if you want to talk through how an interaction with your mother-in-law went and how to adjust for next time, but your partner won't? If he tries to sidestep these conversations, recognize that there might be a timing issue. Ask when would be a good time to have this conversation, emphasizing its importance for remaining a connected team. It's possible he'll be ready to participate once he's cooled down or gotten his own thoughts in order.

But it's also possible your partner might not be interested in doing this work. If this is the case, I want you to know that many women I work with individually come to me because they want to feel different within themselves. Tap into the powerful behavioral strategy of modeling. If you can set boundaries, you can model what this looks like to your partner. Sometimes your husband might be able to learn to do it for himself by watching your example. As you change, there is an opportunity for your partner to change. When you can continue to show what it means to communicate differently, not get stuck in the triangle, and assert your boundaries in a loving and respectful way, your partner may over time also start to see the benefit of this.

THE POWER OF TAKING ACTION

Let's return to Evie and Geoff, who were dealing with Geoff's parents providing abundant support for Geoff's sister's kids but none for Geoff's. Having completed the last step of the VAULT method, Taking Action, they were now armed with a plan moving forward. Geoff allowed himself to feel angry with his mother's choices, seeing the impact it had on his family. Evie supported Geoff in texting his mother and building assertive conversations around his needs. The more he addressed the issue, the more Geoff began to feel empowered by expressing what he needed from his mother.

While his mother agreed to care for the kids more, she never acknowledged that her behavior toward him was any different from her behavior toward his sister. Geoff realized it was not his job to convince her of this, so he and Evie decided that they wouldn't keep having these conversations with his mother. Instead, they leaned into seeing her when it worked for them and preparing themselves for the questions that came from their kids when they asked why they couldn't have more time with their grandmother. As a couple, they found being able to talk openly with each other after seeing his mother to be essential to helping them feel like a cohesive family on the same team.

Chapter 10

PUTTING IT
INTO PRACTICE

But, Dr. Tracy, just tell me how to say it." This is a request I receive every day in both my therapy practice and my online communities. We want to know "the right way" to express ourselves, and while there are no magic words, when I help clients come up with scripts and role-play possible outcomes with them, they often leave the session feeling a sense of renewed power and confidence. They may not know how their situation will ultimately turn out, but they know what their next step is.

Like these clients, you now understand the five steps of the VAULT method, but you probably still have some lingering questions, especially about how to say what you want to say. This chapter will answer those questions and offer scripts to support you. Remember, when another person is respecting our boundaries, we can assert ourselves with them in a warmer, more empathic manner. When they're not respecting our boundaries or are being manipulative or abusive, a firmer, more minimal script makes more sense.

QUESTIONS RELATED TO YOUR HUSBAND'S ACTIONS

Let's start by taking a look at questions about your husband's approach to his relationship with his mother and with you.

How do I air my grievances about my mother-in-law without my husband getting upset at me?

First, recognize that this is your husband's mother. It's natural for him to defend her, especially if he feels you're attacking her character. I discourage couples from venting to each other about the other person's parent, especially if it's become a point of contention, as it probably has for you if you're reading this book.

Instead, build a toolbox of strategies to address your experiences with someone other than your husband. Write out your feelings and reactions to what happened, text a trusted friend, or seek your own therapy support. After airing your feelings, identify what you need. Do you need to be heard and validated? Do you need a solution or plan of action? When you've figured that out, you can share it with your husband, using the "fact plus feeling" formula and state what you need to move forward.

Possible scripts:

* "I need to share something hard with you about your mother, and I need you to just listen."

* "I know it can be difficult to hear negative things about your mom. I'm sharing this with you so that we can move forward in the best possible way."

* "It's not okay to yell at me when I'm trying to share something with you. Can we try again?"

How do I get my husband to stand up for himself?

Before your husband will stand up for himself, he first has to acknowledge that he's being emotionally hurt and that his mother's behavior is damaging your relationship with her. You ultimately can't force your husband to see his mother's behavior or make him change, but if he's ready, you can help facilitate this work. Your husband is used to his mother's actions from lifelong patterns with her, so he might dismiss, minimize, or ignore what she does, believing it's normal or "just how she is." You can help him acknowledge his own experiences with her by asking him what he thought and how he felt when she did or said something. Avoid leading with your own interpretations or experiences (e.g., "Your mother is so rude," "You just let her walk all over you").

Possible scripts:

* "I've noticed that your mother says [X].
  What do you think of that?"

* "Your mom seemed to be quick to express [X].
  How did that feel for you?"

* "I wonder how you would feel if you imagined us
  speaking to our own child that way."

If he recognizes his mother's toxic tendencies, it will require him to assert himself, but he might not know exactly what he wants to assert. Sit down together to talk about what's important and what's possible to communicate using the three A's of taking action in chapter 9. Recognize that it might take a few attempts before he can stand up for himself.

How do I set boundaries when my husband doesn't see them as necessary?

If your husband doesn't see a particular boundary you want to set as necessary, that might be because the boundary has not yet been shared or understood in the context of your needs and values as a couple. These are key pieces to consider, which can be done through the VAULT method. Boundaries are about deciding what is going to be best for *you*. Just because someone else doesn't see them as necessary doesn't make them wrong.

The next question would be how you want to implement a boundary if your partner is not on the same page as you. This all depends on what the boundary is about. For example, you might agree that he accepts food to take home from his mother when he visits solo, but when you are attending, you politely decline the additional meals.

Consider *how* you're expressing your needs with your husband. You will also want to explore self-boundaries and ways to assert your own boundaries independent of your husband.

Possible scripts:

* "This might not be important to you, but it's important to me. I need us to find a solution that's going to work for both of us."

* "I see it this way, and you see it differently. That's okay, and now we need to find a way to move forward that considers both of our needs."

* "Your mother is important to you, and it's part of our values to have her in our life. This is a boundary for me, and I need you to see that it's something I plan to implement."

What do I do if my husband continues to take his mom's side or blames me?

A healthy relationship is about each person understanding the other's perspective and not blaming the other person. Blame and denial of your experience are the continuation of negative communication patterns. Working through the steps of the VAULT method should help you break these patterns. If your husband is struggling with the VAULT method, see Appendix B, which lays out five tips to help him through the process. If the blame and denial continue after working through the VAULT system, it will be important to consider seeking couples therapy. In the meantime, find assertive responses to your husband's blaming statements.

Possible scripts:

* "It's okay to be upset at the situation. It's not okay to blame me."

* "There are multiple people in this dynamic, which means we all play a role in this."

* "I'm not asking you to take sides. I'm asking you to understand what it might be like for me when this happens. Can you try taking my perspective?"

Should I tell my husband the issues that are happening with his mother?

You and your husband are a team, and it's important for you to work together to build and strengthen your family. A dynamic where you don't share things with him is not ideal. However, if what you share focuses on his or his mother's character or how you think he or his mother needs to change, he'll probably feel like you're pushing him against a wall. Instead, focus on problematic behaviors and prioritize your aspirations and values. Use "I feel . . ." statements and connect to what you need. From there, you can find possible solutions. Allow some things to "hang" between the two of you without trying to force a solution when he's not ready.

Possible scripts:

* "Your mom showed up on our doorstep today unannounced. This is difficult because I'm trying to get things done. I need a plan for how we can move forward with drop-ins."

* "It's generous that your mom wants to make these vacation plans with us. I struggle to feel like we have any say in these decisions. I need us to step back and plan what is best for our family first."

* "Your mother insisted our son give her a hug and seemed not to like that I told her no. I would like for us to have a conversation with her about our parenting values."

I stepped out of the triangle. What if my husband asks me for advice on what to do with his mother?

If your husband asks for advice on how to respond to something his mother did, it will be very tempting to put her down. I know that in this position, you want to feel vindicated and seen. You want to put your hands in the air and say, "Finally! You get it!" But this will only put you back in the triangle (as discussed in chapter 7) and keep you all stuck there. Instead of being the problem solver, practice shifting into a supportive and listening role.

Possible scripts:

* "That sounds really difficult. I'm on your side. What do you think you might do next?"

* "Knowing my sensitivity to passive-aggressiveness, which comes from my own mother while growing up, it's really hard for me to watch your mother make these kinds of comments in front of our children. How does this align with what's important to us?"

* "In the past, I've been overly vocal about what hasn't felt good for me with your mom, and I'm realizing that it doesn't really work best for us. I think it's important that you make a choice that feels best for you, and one that comes from our values and aspirations."

What if my husband never sees how his mother's behavior is affecting us?

No matter how clearly you see your MIL's behavior for what it is, your husband might never be able to identify it. If that's the case, refocus on the relationship with your husband and allow him to deal with the relationship with his mother. Work on building acceptance for this part of your husband. When we accept something, we release the desire to change it, to control the outcome, or to justify ourselves. The experience will never be easy or fun, but it is what it is.

Consider finding collaborative ways to approach your husband while also sharing your feelings, which takes the focus away from his mother. Your job is not to prove your feeling to your partner but to ask him to validate your experience.

Possible scripts:

* "I heard your mother say [X]. What did you think of that?"

* "I know your mom tries to help us, but I felt dismissed when she said [X]."

* "I felt hurt when your mom said [X]. Could you validate the hurt that I'm feeling?"

What do I do when my MIL continues to exclude me from family events?

Even if your MIL sees you as an outsider and doesn't want you to go to family events, hopefully your husband sees that you are a team and a "package deal." If he doesn't, you can help him to understand that while you respect his family of origin, it is now time to choose each other. You can also remind him that you are not creating distance and separation from his family but instead trying to feel secure with him. Feeling like you're a team is essential to a healthy marriage.

From here, there are a few things you can decide on. Your

husband might tell his mother, "I will not be attending this event if my wife is not included." Or you might decide that you no longer want to attend these events and you're fine with your husband going without you. The best way to protect your peace might ultimately be accepting that your MIL views you as an outsider. You can also consider what you might say to your MIL if she tells you that you're not part of the family.

Possible scripts:

* "These are hurtful comments. I imagine you wouldn't want that kind of thing said to our own daughter."

* "It's okay if your mother doesn't view me as part of your family. But we are married, and we are a family now."

* "You and I are a family and I need us to be on the same page. I can accept that your mother doesn't see me as part of her family."

QUESTIONS RELATED TO YOUR MARRIAGE

Now that we've answered some questions about your husband's actions, let's turn to questions about your marriage.

How do I deal with an MIL who inserts herself into our marriage or a husband who tells his mom about our marriage?
Unless you are experiencing emotional or physical abuse, the details of your marriage need to stay within your marriage. This protects your bond. When your MIL gets involved in your relationship—or when your husband involves her—this strengthens the unhealthy triangle dynamic and weakens all of your dyad bonds.

Possible scripts to use with your MIL:

* "I appreciate your concern about our marriage. Our relationship is not on the table to talk about."

* "Please refrain from making comments about our relationship. It isn't helpful."

Possible scripts to use with your husband:

* "I know you're trying to get support about the struggles that we're having. When you turn to your mother, it actually weakens our relationship with her, and she ends up viewing me as the bad guy. Please keep the details of our marriage between us."

* "I appreciate you wanting to seek support from your mother. However, it hurts our marriage when you share our private details with her. Is there a friend or therapist you can speak to instead?"

How do we deal with in-laws overstaying their visit or expecting us to be available or in contact more frequently than we want to?

If your in-laws have unrealistic expectations about the length and frequency of the time you spend together, you'll need to set boundaries and ensure that you act on the consequences when those boundaries aren't respected. If they stay longer than you agreed to, you ask them to leave. If they ask you to attend another family dinner, you politely decline. Remember it is not your job to meet their expectations. While your MIL can expect more visits, this might not be possible for you. I also like to give a potential positive interpretation: While it might feel like your in-laws don't respect your time, it's possible that they truly just don't understand the reality of your schedule. You might benefit from helping them understand all that's on your plate.

Possible scripts:

* "You can visit today, but we only have an hour. At that point, we will ask you to leave."

* "I know you'd like us to visit more often. This is a busy season for us, so we won't be able to attend weekly dinners. We would love to schedule a monthly one so it's in the calendar."

* "We loved having you stay with us last time. For this visit, we can only have you stay for four days. Which days would you like to choose?"

What should my husband do when his mother complains about me behind my back?

When your MIL complains about you to your husband, she is reinforcing the triangle and thereby weakening her bond not only with her son but also with you. Given that she's speaking to your husband, he needs to be the one to assert his boundary with her, stating that this behavior is not appropriate. What is appropriate is for his mother to process her own feelings with her own peers, siblings, friends, or therapist. Ultimately, your husband needs to understand that allowing her to "vent" or say things about you behind your back impacts everyone.

Possible scripts for you to use with your husband:

* "I know your mom likes to talk to you about these things. However, this is hurtful, and it doesn't help us build family and connection. I need you to tell her to stop saying things behind my back."

* "This behavior doesn't help you and me feel close with your mom. I need you to tell her to bring her concerns directly to me, or to go and work on them herself."

* "This isn't the kind of thing a mother should be sharing with her son. She needs to speak to someone else."

Possible scripts for your husband to use with his mother:

* "Mom, this kind of conversation isn't helpful for my marriage. This is my wife. Please do not speak about her behind her back."

* "I get that you're upset about this. If you have a problem with [name], you need to address it with her."

* "When you say things like that about my wife, I will change the topic."

How do I deal with my MIL when she makes our life moments about her?

When your MIL makes milestones like your wedding or your pregnancy about her, it can be painful, especially if you'd hoped she could celebrate you. When I hear of MILs doing this, I question whether they know how to deal with deeper feelings of insecurity related to their own importance in their family. They may also be self-focused, and making it about themselves is their way of dealing with discomfort. Your MIL might lack awareness that she's doing this, and pointing it out might only lead her to become defensive. You can, however, approach her with a statement about your own needs, such as a request to be seen or validated separately. But be prepared: No matter how eloquently you communicate it, she might not be able to meet you with what you need.

Possible scripts:

* "I know how excited you are about our pregnancy. I need us to celebrate this in a different way. It would feel better to . . ."

* "When we talk about our baby, we've noticed that you compare our experience to your new puppy. This doesn't feel good, and we need you to stop comparing these experiences."

* "We know you're happy for us. We would appreciate you celebrating our accomplishment without shifting the spotlight."

QUESTIONS RELATED TO PARENTING AND CHILDREN

Relations with your mother-in-law can get especially tricky once you have kids of your own. Let's look at common questions about what to do if she tries to criticize or interfere with your parenting.

What should we do when my MIL questions our parenting choices?

Given the changes in parenting styles over the years, there is often some intergenerational conflict and confusion about "what works." You will parent in the way that you think is best, which is probably different from what your in-laws and your own parents did. When your MIL questions your parenting choices, is she asking from a place of genuine interest and curiosity or a place of judgment and criticism? It's important to know the difference and check her intentions.

When these questions come from a place of judgment, what tends to happen is that you end up arguing with your MIL about why you made the choices that you did. But giving her a lengthy rationale implicitly concedes that you owe her an explanation and gives her permission to continue to question your choices. The goal, instead, is not to enter into these conversations if she is not approaching you with curiosity, and to have a firm boundary with yourself that you will not provide details on your parenting choices.

Possible scripts:

* "It makes sense that you did it differently. This is what works best for our family."

* "I know you're coming from a good place. We're flooded by parenting advice and would prefer if you just told us we're doing a good job."

* "It's not helpful to receive parenting advice. Please refrain from sharing it."

My MIL wants to be more involved with our kids. I don't want her to be. How do I address this?

If your MIL is asking to be more involved with your kids, it's important to first understand what she means by "more involved." What does this look like in terms of daily, weekly, or monthly visits? What does "being involved" give her? Is it about connecting with your kids, or is it about receiving attention and feeling special? If the latter, while you don't need to invite her to be involved when you don't want to, one approach might be to create special time-limited moments with her. Perhaps you meet at a park for an hour while the kids play, or invite her along on an outing so she can participate.

You ultimately get to choose how involved your MIL is with your family. It is not your job to meet her desires. She had her turn to be a parent, and now you have yours. Return to your values (chapter 5) and aspirations (chapter 6) to center yourself in what is important to you and what you desire from your relationship with family.

Possible scripts:

* "I know you'd like to be included in this. This is something that we'll be doing just the three of us."

* "I see you're upset you weren't invited for this. I get it."

* "You play an important role as a grandma. This amount of time together is what works for us right now."

I want my MIL to be more involved with our kids. How do I express my frustrations about her lack of help?

In contrast to those who want their MILs to be less involved, others would love more support from their MILs, especially with childcare. If this is you, be curious about your expectations of your MIL and what you saw modeled to you; your MIL might have a different understanding of her role in your family. With some MILs, you can solve the problem with a clear invitation to step in to help you. But if she's the type of person who keeps her distance, you might need to move into acceptance for who she is and do any necessary grieving for the involved MIL you wish you had. Remember, though, that relationships change. As you and your family grow, she might begin to show up differently.

Possible scripts:

* "We love the time you spend with us. Would you like to join us again next weekend?"

* "I know you've been busy with all that's going on. We would love to have you spend more time together. Is this something we could talk about?"

* "I know you don't want to feel intrusive, but I could really use your help with this weekend's family meal. Could you bring the dessert?"

How do I address when my MIL compares her involvement to my own mother's involvement?

A hard reality that I've seen repeatedly is that many women are closer to their own mothers than to their MILs, which is especially true after the birth of a child. For some, this isn't the case, and they find comfort and closeness with their MIL. What's important in the dynamic with your MIL is recognizing that your relationship with her *will* be different from your relationship with your own mom. You likely feel more comfortable with your mother, so in hard parenting moments you reach out to her automatically. You have decades of establishing boundaries and saying no to your mother, so setting boundaries with her about her role as grandmother might feel easier. You can more easily ask your mother for help with caring for the kids.

I remind couples that the husband needs to take responsibility for communicating and keeping his kids in touch with his mother, just as the wife is responsible for communicating and keeping them in touch with hers. This is important in maintaining the family bond. How this is done is up to you and him to decide, but it is important that he keep his mother in the loop. Remember, you can validate your MIL's feeling, even if you don't agree with her or believe that anything has to change.

Possible scripts:

* "Please don't compare yourself to my mom. You each play different roles, and you're both important to us. I hope you can see that."

* "I understand this is upsetting for you."

* "You're right. I am closer to my mom, so I do tend to call her more regularly and seek out her advice. Perhaps we can find some other times for you to visit us."

How do I deal with my MIL playing favorites with grandkids?

This type of question comes up frequently, and I've worked with several women who don't like how their MIL treats their children compared with how she treats her other grandkids. Giving your MIL a positive interpretation first, let's assume she is not aware she's doing this. She might be acting without intention, as many people do, or she might have her own experiences going on (e.g., perhaps she worries she's being intrusive with you, so she steps back). Avoid telling your MIL that she's playing favorites, as she will likely receive that as an accusation and get defensive. Instead, reframe the question to focus on identifying what you or your child needs.

Possible scripts:

* "We noticed that you spend a lot of time with the other grandkids. We would love to have you share time with our kids too. Do you have any ideas for how we can support that happening?"

* "Our children have noticed that their cousins seem to get more gifts than they do. I was wondering what you thought of that and how we might also consider our kids' feelings when they're with you."

When it comes to treating people respectfully, you are still your child's parent. You can model what it means to build healthy relationships and assertiveness by communicating in front of your children.

Possible scripts:

* "Hey, Grandma, it doesn't feel good for our kids to be compared to their cousins. Please don't do that."

* "It's important that our children feel important too. If you're giving gifts to the other kids, please consider our kids as well."

If you receive a defensive response, this suggests that she might not be able to hear your concerns. Ultimately, if your MIL doesn't change her behavior, you can switch to focusing on helping your child process their feelings and grieve their unmet desires for grandparents, recognizing that they don't get to change or choose their grandparents.

How do I navigate the relationship between my child and my MIL?

Responsibility for the relationship between a grandparent and a grandchild flows downward; a grandparent is responsible for the relationship with their grandchild. It is not okay for a grandparent to say to a child, "Why don't you call me?" or "You never visit Grandma." Additionally, many parents today reject the outdated message "You have to give Grandma a hug goodbye," wanting to teach their kids the values of bodily autonomy and consent instead. You can facilitate your child's availability and the overall environment, but ultimately the ways in which your MIL interacts with her grandchild will be up to her. As the primary decision-maker for your kids, it's your job to help them talk about their experiences with Grandma and cope with their feelings. As parents, we can help our kids build the skills to assert their needs to their grandmother.

If you notice that your MIL tries to guilt-trip your child, you can approach this in a few ways: You can help your child learn what to say in those moments, you can ask to use your voice to speak for them and assert a boundary, or you can speak to your MIL and your child after the event.

Possible scripts:

* "Grandma, it doesn't feel good when you say that."

* "Grandma, we don't make comments about bodies. That's not helpful."

* "Hey, Grandma, it's [child's name]'s choice to decide to hug you or not."

We're about to have a baby, and I'm worried about what this will look like with my MIL. Help!

If you're expecting a baby and wondering how it will impact your relationship with your MIL, I'm so glad you're reading this book! Be sure to read chapters 5 and 6 and talk about your parenting values and aspirations with your partner, including what you hope for in terms of your MIL's involvement. Once you have an idea of this, have an open conversation with your MIL to share what your wishes are. The more specific you are about your needs and desires and her expectations, the more you'll all be on the same page. Here are some top items to consider at this stage:

* What "help" really means to you and how your in-laws can support you during this time.

* How often and for how long your in-laws should visit and where they'll stay when they do.

* What fairness looks like between the two sides of the families (things will never be exactly equal).

* Their expectations and your boundaries around visiting your newborn (e.g., no kisses to the baby's mouth, hands, or feet).

* How announcements are made and what can be shared on social media.

All of this can change depending on what you need once you welcome your baby. Flexibility is key. At this point, you are trying to make implicit needs explicit.

Possible scripts:

* "For our time in the hospital, we're asking for no visitors. We'll let you know when we're home and ready for a visit."

* "We would like to be the ones to announce the arrival of our baby. Please do not post anything on social media or tell others our news."

* "We would love for you to be able to visit and spend time with us. We'll want to ensure we find our own routine as well, so we ask that visits be short over the first three months."

* "We're excited for you to become Grandma. It's important that we have your support in the choices that we make. We aren't looking for parenting advice."

QUESTIONS ABOUT OTHER ISSUES WITH YOUR MIL

There are many other specific issues that people experience with their mother-in-law that perhaps we haven't yet covered. Let's tackle them now.

My MIL wants to share all our information on social media and doesn't respect our privacy. How do we talk to her about this?
Let's start with a positive interpretation: Many people from older generations genuinely don't understand younger generations' standards for what should and should not be shared on social media. They haven't learned yet! You are in charge of what you want and don't want shared on social media, and it's not okay for them to violate that, but sometimes a little education goes a long way. Explain, clearly and concisely, that sharing private information can make it easier for accounts to get hacked, for identities to be stolen, and for photos to be seen by people they weren't intended for. If your MIL still doesn't comply, you might choose to withhold certain information from her. This might not be how you hoped to show up in your relationship with your MIL, but it might be necessary if she won't respect your privacy.

Possible scripts:

* "We do not want you sharing images of us and our children on social media. Please remove the photos you posted."

* "We noticed you posted photos of the kids when we asked you not to. We won't be sending you photos again if you keep posting them."

* "You told Aunt Patty that we had a miscarriage. This isn't something we're sharing with other people. In the future, please do not share our private information with others."

My MIL likes to gossip about other family members and complain about her marriage to me. What can I say to make her stop?

Research shows that when a mother-in-law gossips or vents about other family members to her daughter-in-law, the relationship between DIL and MIL is negatively affected.[1] Even if she means well, this behavior leads you to question what she says about you behind your back and weakens your trust. These are valid reasons to disengage from gossip, even if it is accepted as part of the family's culture.

Possible scripts:

* "I love our conversations, but let's focus on things that are happening for us instead of talking about others."

* "I don't feel comfortable talking about others. I'm going to change the topic, and next time, please refrain from bringing up others' private information."

* Do not respond to your MIL's gossip and change the topic.

What can I do with an MIL who believes I "stole" her son?

When an MIL believes her DIL "stole" her son, this tells me that she struggles with the idea of individuation and feels scared of losing her role in the family. Of course, the truth is that her son was never "hers," as people are not possessions. It's not your job to convince her that you didn't steal her son. Instead, you and your husband can find ways of including her in your life that work best for you. Remember that we can always validate someone's emotional experience even if we don't agree with them.

Possible scripts:

* With humor: "You're right! I do take up much of his attention now. You'll always be his mother."

* With empathy for the feeling: "It makes sense to feel a shift in your relationship, and that's hard for a mother."

* With firm redirection: "That's not what has happened, and that kind of statement isn't helpful for us."

How do I approach my MIL about things she's doing that I find annoying?

It's human to feel annoyed by another person! When you view your MIL's actions as annoying, it can speak to your own perceptions and needs. Depending on your history and the baggage you bring to this dynamic, you might be getting stuck in a common unhelpful thinking pattern called *confirmation bias*. This is where we only take in information that confirms a preexisting belief. If you think your MIL is annoying or intrusive, you'll only see the moments when she's being annoying and intrusive and forget about the ones where she's being supportive and helpful.

When you're annoyed, ask yourself, "What would an outsider think?," "What is a more neutral way of viewing this?," and "What is the most reasonable response to this kind of behavior?"

Is there space to practice letting go of those negative perceptions and building more neutrality? You don't have to aim for outright positivity, and you certainly don't have to become best friends with your MIL, but try to see irritating statements and behavior just for what they are: neutral.

If you do decide that your MIL's behavior is impacting your ability to have a relationship with her, be sure to revisit chapter 8 to work through your boundaries.

Possible scripts:

* When she is "helping" after you've told her not to: "I can tell how much you love to help. Please sit down and allow me to do this."

* When she says something inappropriate: "That doesn't feel good, and I would prefer that you not make those kinds of comments in front of me."

* When she drops off gifts for the kids: "You love giving gifts to the kids. We've talked to you before about dropping off things for the kids. It ends up feeling overwhelming for us. We really need you to just show up as you are and give attention to the kids. We will accept the gifts this time, but next time, please don't bring anything."

Help! My MIL lives with me, and we're struggling to have a harmonious relationship.

Bringing together adults of different generations can be challenging as you try to navigate freedom, control over space, and autonomy. It can be a recipe for disaster if implicit expectations and desires are not openly discussed in order to reach agreements as a cohesive unit. You'll need to decide whether you're including your live-in MIL in household decisions or if she's living as a guest in your home. You'll also want to clearly define the roles you each play in housecleaning, meal preparation and planning, and parenting and discipline. Discuss what time you expect to spend together and what time you expect to spend apart, whether this is through meals, individual activities, or friends outside the home; many couples agree to do something separate from their live-in parent one night a week.

Ultimately, the main reason couples struggle in this area is that they didn't lay out expectations and desires clearly, or if they did, they didn't take action to enforce the relevant boundaries. Now is the opportunity to have these conversations. Although they're uncomfortable in the moment, they can make family life much more harmonious in the long run.

Possible scripts:

* "We've been having a hard time seeing eye to eye. Let's sit down on Sunday to plan out what is working for us and what we need to change."

* "It seems like we're struggling to coexist in the home. We both want to feel comfortable. Let's bring forward some ideas of what we can do to help you feel more comfortable and what you can do to participate."

* "I know living in our home is not the same as living in your own home. This is how we do X. But when it comes to Y, I would love to have you take over."

How do I address cultural differences with my MIL?

Many differences can show up between MILs and DILs— cultural, generational, religious, the list goes on. Ultimately, you and your husband get to choose how you will structure your family, keeping in mind that there is no "right" way. I know this goes against the grain for many cultures, in which case there will likely be extra discomfort.

Consider learning more about the meaning behind your MIL's cultural traditions and seeing where you can walk beside your MIL and where you want to diverge from her. If your husband wants to continue to follow certain practices, it will be important to understand why: Is it truly important to him, or is it about keeping his mother happy? Remember, it's not your job to keep your parents happy.

Possible scripts:

* "I know how important your culture is to you. We're choosing to do something different, and we can appreciate that this is upsetting."

* "We'd love to know how we can honor your cultural practices, but we also want to explore having our own traditions that might be different from yours."

* "We want to continue to have a strong relationship with you. Doing so doesn't mean that we have to do the same things as you, even though I know this might feel difficult for you."

How do I heal these old wounds from my MIL? I recognize that she won't change, but I'm still hurting.
You've been hurt. You had hopes and desires for a relationship with your MIL, for who she could be and the role she could play. Allow yourself to grieve that loss. Grief and loss require us to make space for all emotions, including anger, denial, bargaining, sadness, and acceptance. Write a letter to your MIL, but rip it up and don't give it to her. Allow yourself to feel your feelings through the writing process. Sentences might start with "I'm angry because . . ." or "When you said [X], I felt deeply hurt because . . ."

Some people choose to share something with their MIL about the hurt they have experienced. There isn't anything wrong with letting someone know how they've impacted you, but check your expectations for what that person can offer. Be prepared for your MIL to react with defensiveness, denial, or an inability to understand how she has impacted you.

My MIL asks my husband to bring the kids to visit her without me. Should we just see family separately?
When your husband and kids visit his side of the family, you don't necessarily have to come along. Some couples decide to visit their extended families separately. While this solves the short-term problem of having to deal with your MIL, it might create other challenges, so revisit your values and aspirations before making a decision. For some DILs, not attending family get-togethers further entrenches the narrative that they're "not part of this family" and creates more problems over time. For others, it provides a healthy opportunity for your MIL to step into a supportive role by helping to care for the kids or having more one-on-one time with her son.

If you do decide to nurture family relationships separately, be sure to protect the "we" bond between you and your partner. Encourage him to do the following:

* Speak only positively about you.

* Share only news that you've both previously agreed you're open to sharing (e.g., "We've been teaching our kids how to ride a bike" or "We're doing some home renovations").

* Stand up for you if his mother makes negative comments about you (e.g., "Please don't speak about my wife that way," "I'm not going to engage in conversations about my partner").

* Hold off on making commitments and decisions without first speaking to you (e.g., "That's an interesting idea. We'll have to talk about it and get back to you").

* Use "we" language when talking about decisions made as a couple (e.g., shift from "Sarah doesn't want to visit for the holidays" or "Sarah is choosing to exclusively breastfeed" to "We won't be able to visit for the holidays" and "We're choosing to exclusively breastfeed").

Additionally, ask your partner to avoid the following:

* Taking his mother's side when she makes negative comments about you, even if it's about something that the two of you are struggling with in your partnership.

* Conversations that put you in the middle or make you out to be the "bad" one (e.g., if she says, "Your wife probably doesn't want me to feed your kids candy," he can say, "Actually, Mom, that's something that we both agree on").

* Not mentioning you at all. This makes it seem like you aren't part of the family, maintaining your status as an "outsider" and creating a triangle with you or her in the middle.

* Talking about your marital difficulties with his mother. This also goes for any other topics like finances or parenting decisions that you've agreed to keep between you.

I've tried to improve my relationship with my MIL, but nothing is changing. Should we go no-contact?

With the rise of information about generational trauma and breaking cycles, many people are choosing to cut contact with family members who are abusive, manipulative, or emotionally harmful. Going no-contact might entail not seeing, texting, or speaking to each other for a finite period of time, or it might be a permanent estrangement. Anyone who chooses the no-contact route has likely withstood a long history of emotional neglect and/or abuse. While you might reach a pivotal moment, you've likely experienced death by a thousand paper cuts. Perhaps no matter what you try with your MIL, her behavior has stayed the same or gotten worse, or she's unwilling to consider your feelings and keeps adding fuel to the fire.

Only you and your partner can make this choice together, and it's one to consider carefully. If you do come to this decision, I recommend not "ghosting" family members, which only adds more distress and unrest. Instead, communicate what has happened by sharing the facts (i.e., behaviors and actions), your feelings about the facts, and your decision to move forward. While this conversation can trigger others to be defensive, to blame you or your marriage, or to rise to a new level of vitriol, it's still important to let them know where you stand. However uncomfortable it is, this conversation is about asserting your needs and wishes going forward.

If you go no-contact with your MIL, other family members (such as a sibling, an aunt or uncle, or your FIL) will likely try to change your mind about it. These attempts are often fueled by their own unconscious fear and desire to preserve the family dynamic's status quo. They might see only the precipitating event and not the years of mistreatment that have led you to make this decision. These family members don't need to approve of or like your choice, and they don't get to make it for you.

When considering going no-contact, come back to your values and what is important to you as a family. If you value knowing older generations and having your children know their blood relatives, you might consider going low-contact. This means that you and your husband limit the amount of contact and frequency with your in-laws, finding a level of tolerability that will feel best for you. You'll want to reevaluate when, where, and how you engage with your MIL. What do visits look like? Are they for family events or anytime someone wants a visit? Where will the visits take place? You might decide to shorten visit lengths or stay in an Airbnb or hotel instead of sleeping at your in-laws' house. You will also want to consider boundaries around conversations and actions together. If boundaries are more likely to be crossed sitting in your MIL's kitchen, consider meeting at a coffee shop or seeing a movie with the kids; it's often easier to keep things pleasant in a neutral, public space.

The situation hasn't improved. Should I get a divorce?

This is a question that I'm asked when people feel completely stuck and nothing has changed. No one wants to get a divorce. If you're asking this, you've probably been struggling for a while, and you've likely tolerated some very hurtful behavior. I remind people that no one can tell you whether you should stay or go, because no one lives the daily moments in your marriage or the interactions that have unfolded with your MIL. Only you know your experiences and your truth.

Of course, I advise going to couples therapy and using strategies like the ones in this book, but if you're considering a divorce, I imagine you have tried everything possible. The unfortunate truth is that many people do get to a place where they no longer feel any safety, respect, or trust in their marriage, and they want something different in their life. If you've truly decided that you will leave unless something changes, you can communicate that to your partner, but only do so if you're seriously considering ending the relationship. Otherwise, such ultimatums become empty threats that break the trust in a marriage.

I hope you can find a path forward in your marriage that feels right for you. But if that's not possible, please know that you're not alone, and choosing to divorce doesn't make you a bad person (or a bad parent). Prioritizing you is an act of courage.

FIND YOUR BEST APPROACH

When it comes to dealing with your MIL, there will never be a one-size-fits-all response. Your relationship with her, as well as your needs, will be different from others' relationships and needs. So while the answers to these questions are one approach, be sure to check in with yourself to see how they feel for you and what would be best to implement for you and your husband. Remind yourself that entering into uncomfortable conversations will allow you to make changes for yourself—but it doesn't ensure that the other person is going to change.

A FINAL WORD

Congratulations! You've reached the end of *You, Your Husband, and His Mother*. You've grappled with the dynamics at play in your family of origin and your husband's, and you've focused on getting on the same team with him. You've worked through the VAULT method, identifying your values and aspirations, understanding your triangle, setting limits and boundaries, and taking action on everything you learned. I hope this works for you as I've seen it work for so many of my clients, and that you're able to forge a more peaceful and positive relationship with your mother-in-law.

One of the most powerful realizations my clients tell me they have when doing this work is that the dynamic in their in-laws' family existed before they got there. It also becomes freeing when you realize your MIL is responsible for her own decisions, emotions, and actions. She can have her own wishes, but you don't have to make them all come true. You can't change your MIL or even make her *want* to change. These aha moments remove the blame and shame my clients feel and provide them with a new perspective of their MIL and their husband. They can do the work they need to do without feeling like a victim or a villain.

Creating a healthy marriage and family is a journey, and one that requires you to enter into hard conversations, accept that you cannot control and change others, and be willing to break old cycles. You and your husband being on the same page is imperative for the future of your marriage; you need to have those challenging discussions. It's my hope that you and your husband will keep finding each other through all your challenges and continue to be a team.

This book is built to be a resource for you to come back to time and time again. While no two stories or journeys will look the same, the steps in the VAULT method are a guide for making choices—for you, your marriage, and your family. When you choose to courageously make a change, you end up living a more meaningful and connected life with a relationship that feels more aligned with who you are and where you want to go.

I am cheering you on. For the work you are doing to heal old wounds—and for bravely breaking old cycles for your marriage and family.

YOUR NEXT MOVE

*C*hange is powerful, and it doesn't happen in silos but in community. I'm so glad you're part of this community! The fact that you read this book tells me your relationship is important to you and you're ready to keep having insights and making shifts toward a lasting connection.

You can continue to strengthen your relationship in my online program, Be Connected, where you'll find a library of bite-size lessons, guides, and downloadable worksheets to help you learn all the skills and tools I teach my couples every day in my therapy room. You'll tackle issues like getting on the same page as parents, redistributing the mental load, and communicating based on your attachment styles. Plus you'll be part of a community of people who are doing the same work—breaking old cycles and healing wounds so they can have a lifetime of love.

I can't wait to see you there!

DrTracyD.com/join

ACKNOWLEDGMENTS

To the thousands of people who have shared their stories with me, sought my advice, and needed to know they were not alone in their relational struggles—you have my deepest gratitude. Thank you for your courage and vulnerability while doing this work alongside me. Writing a book is about our collective stories and experiences, and because of you, I have been able to bring this resource to help you build the relationships you desire—in your marriage and your families.

The work I get to do every day is made possible because of my biggest supporter and husband, Greg. You help me break through my self-imposed limits and encourage me to reach for more. Whether in my career or on the ski hill, you nudge me toward growth and remind me to embrace discomfort. I'm so grateful for the way you always hold my hand through it all.

To my children, Anderson and Eloise. It is a gift to be your mother. You challenge me to play more, to express more, and to be daring in all that I do. When I told you I was writing another book, you simply said, "It's okay, we've done this before." That was the permission slip I needed—not only to be your mother but also to be a writer. I love you both so much.

Cecilia Lyra, you believed in me and my writing from the first day we met. Thank you for the extra notes of validation, your confidence in my work, and guiding me through living out my dreams of being an author. Lauren O'Neal, your enthusiasm for this project from the very beginning has meant the world to me. Your careful attention to detail and ability to refine my words have been invaluable. Thank you for your care and dedication to helping bring this book to life. Thank you to the entire Tarcher team for getting this book into the hands of so many! Thank you, Nicola Wheir, for helping me bring clarity and focus to my ideas and ensuring this book communicates its message in the best possible way.

To my family, who have continued to support us as we live in a separate city: Thank you for supporting my work, our kids, and both me and Greg on all of our adventures. To my parents, you taught me early on what it means to stand up for each other. Thank you for supporting my dreams of becoming a psychologist and writer.

To my friends, who are my secure bases in all that I do—thank you, not just for your support but for also telling everyone else about the work I'm doing. Melissa and Meagan, I treasure our "family room" consultations and your encouragement as I navigate this path of my work. Ashleigh, your daily support across every aspect of my life—books, business, and beyond—means the world to me. Nicole, we will always have our conversations in Portugal while celebrating our ten-year wedding anniversaries with our husbands. Your brilliance and joy for my work have been a gift. Madeline and Chelsea, building meaningful friendships as mothers is no small feat, yet you've made connection and vulnerability easy. Thank you for your trust and your time during my writing weekends.

I am surrounded by so many amazing women who work alongside me in different roles, including my colleagues at Integrated Wellness and the members of my Be Connected Digital team. Thank you for working beside me, for your connection, and for your support to make this all possible.

To my clients, who trust me with their most vulnerable stories. Thank you for choosing me to do this work with, allowing me to witness your courage, vulnerability, and growth. Your stories and your openness matter to me.

To my online friends, the ones who share the social media space with me, who send me voice notes, who check in, who support my work and have shared this book—thank you! I didn't know I would get to meet so many amazing people when I started doing this work, and I am glad we have had the chance to connect.

I am grateful for all of you in my online community. We have been on such an amazing journey together over the past seven years. Your DMs, your shares, and your comments. The moments of turning to your partner and saying, "Dr. Tracy says . . ." The breaking of cycles and creating meaningful family connections. I love knowing that I get to be part of this work with you, learning how to connect in a different way with both your husbands and your families. I will continue to be here to support you on your journey!

Finally, to you, dear reader. I hope this book meets you wherever you are in the work you are doing. Thank you for trusting me to be part of your journey.

Appendix A

YOUR TRANSITION TO BEING A MOTHER-IN-LAW

As you think more deeply about what goes into a good relationship between mother-in-law and daughter-in-law, you may start to wonder what you can do to facilitate such a relationship when you become an MIL yourself someday. Many women reach out to me expressing their desire to be a good MIL and maintain a positive relationship with their adult child. Some express fear given their own difficult experiences, while others express joy and excitement. I want you to know this: The fact that you picked up this book already tells me that you want something different, that you recognize the importance of boundaries and breaking cycles. You've done so much great work already! Here's how to keep up that work when you transition to being an MIL.

We often default to autopilot in our relationships, lacking reflection on what is meaningful and important. To make sure you're consciously considering your role as MIL, answer the following questions:

* What three words would I use to describe the family
  I want?

* What three words would I like my adult child and their partner to use to describe me?

* What situations or events might I struggle with in this transition?

* Knowing the ways I communicate and cope with my feelings, what challenges might arise when things change?

To help you build a healthy, connected family, consider these three principles: inclusivity, flexibility, and responsibility. *Inclusivity* means viewing your adult child's partner not as an outsider but as part of a "we." An "us versus them" mentality breeds resentment and stress—for you *and* for your adult child. *Flexibility* might include accepting new ways of spending time together, celebrating holidays, or offering support. It might even include being flexible about your expectations of who you thought would join your family. Finally, *responsibility* means taking ownership of nurturing the relationship with your adult child and their partner. Responsibility is about seeing how you contribute to what happens and being willing to repair mistakes. I like to remind people to "rotate the room" and consider what the person sitting across from you might be experiencing. Remember that a "close family" isn't defined by spending a certain amount of time together. There are many ways a family can be healthy and connected.

You will have feelings about the person your adult child chooses as their partner. You may or may not hit it off right away. As you get to know them more, you might find parts of them that you like or don't like, or you may discover that they have different ways of approaching life. Either way, practicing differentiation will be an ongoing skill with both your adult child and their partner. They are allowed to be different from you, and you can still have a good relationship with each of them.

Accepting your child's partner is incredibly important for healthy in-law relationships. This means that you see that you cannot control your adult child or make this choice for them. You do not have to be their partner's best friend, but you can still be respectful. Criticizing your child's partner or trying to create a divide between them will only push your child away from you.

THREE PHASES TO BECOMING THE MIL YOU WANT TO BE

Over years of clinical practice, I've identified three different phases in the transition to being a mother-in-law. In each phase, there is work you can do to become the MIL you want to be.

PHASE 1:
WELCOMING

In the first phase, you're getting to know who your child has chosen as a partner and welcoming them to the family. The strategies below are important for maintaining an open, trusting, and respectful relationship with both your child and their partner.

* Encourage autonomy. This phase requires you to continue to create healthy separation and individuation from your adult child. This means appreciating that they have their own thoughts, feelings, opinions, values, and desires. They will do things differently from you, and they might not have all the same values you have. Honor these differences.

* Practice curiosity. Ask open-ended questions and learn about the experiences your adult child has in their relationship as well as who their partner is. One MIL described this phase as a "season of fun," like getting to know a new friend. Curiosity requires you to be open and nonjudgmental. Remember the years between you and your kids—they're going to act and look different from you!

* Nurture your identity. There will likely be a change in how often your adult child contacts you or asks for support. This is normal as they start to seek that support from another person in their life. This is a great time for you to look at what sparks joy for you and do more of it. Avoid blaming your child's partner for decreased contact.

* Practice using active listening, genuine concern, and asking if your adult child and their partner want advice.[1] It's not too early to ask them what feels supportive and what feels hurtful or overinvolved.

PHASE 2:
BUILDING

In this phase, your adult child is becoming more serious with their chosen partner. The strategies below will help you remain curious and open about your child's partner and relationship.

* Accept the decisions the couple makes together. See your adult child's actions as stemming from the couple's collective choices, not from their partner's choices alone. Avoid making their partner the scapegoat.

* Instead of making assumptions, ask more questions to understand their choices.

* Break cycles. Recognize when you're defaulting to old scripts, such as putting your needs before theirs in situations where it's not appropriate. You can choose to do something different.

* Avoid the authority role. You don't need to tell your child and their partner "how things are." Instead, ask what works for them. Trust that they'll figure out what they need to.

Become an ally. Have their backs, without dictating their lives.

* Communicate needs and desires clearly, while also appreciating that in any relationship, needs and desires cannot always be met.

* Nurture the individual relationships. Depending on the relationship you have with your adult child and their partner, find a balance between one-on-one time and time with them as a unit. While not every child-in-law will want the individual time with you, it is important to recognize that you need to build an adult relationship with them.

* Remain flexible. Connection is not defined by spending a set amount of time together but rather by sharing experiences, validating and supporting each other, and being willing to problem solve when difficult moments arrive.

* Accept that you might not be kept in the loop on everything. Many parents feel they have a right to know about upcoming changes like engagements or family planning. While it can feel painful not to be informed of these things, remember that it's not done maliciously.

* As your child's relationship with their partner deepens, continue to support the partner as part of the family. Avoid treating them differently from other family members or placing different expectations on them.

* Recognize what's appropriate to share and what's not. With both your adult child and their partner, you shouldn't disclose details about your marriage or the private information of other family members. Even if you feel close with them, it's not their job to provide this kind of

emotional support to you. Seek support from other family members, friends, or a therapist.

PHASE 3:
DEEPENING

Your adult child and their partner are now making moves to build their own family, perhaps with a milestone like moving in together, getting engaged, getting married, or welcoming a baby. These changes can bring feelings of excitement for you, but they can also bring uncertainty about your role changing in your child's life. The strategies below will help you navigate these feelings successfully.

* Remember that you have played a special role in contributing to who your child is today as an adult. It is not your child's job to please you or to make you feel important. Self-esteem has to come from within.

* Allow yourself space to grieve the changes that are happening in your family (e.g., your role is changing, holiday traditions are changing). Holding the *both-and* is an important part in the parenthood journey; you can be both sad that your child is growing up *and* happy that you're watching them become an adult.

* Practice seeing your adult child's autonomy as healthy and not as an indication that they're excluding you. It's helpful to practice depersonalization: "This isn't *about* me." A healthy relationship doesn't just allow your child to "leave" their family of origin—it requires it. They need the autonomy to create their own family.

* Communicate openly with your child-in-law about your relationship with them. Share your experience with your

own MIL and talk about what you hope to do to continue to nurture your relationship with your child-in-law. Give an open invitation to revisit difficult moments and be willing to enter into these hard conversations when they arise.

* Redefine ways of creating family time. When we lose flexibility in defining time together, more tension is created. Explore with your child and their partner what time together looks like. Ask them, "How do you want me to play a role in your life?" and "What can I do to support you both during this time?"

* Be open to solving conflict and talking about hard things. View this as an exercise to heal relationships but not to change the other person.

* See needs, boundaries, and choices as coming from both your child and their partner, not just from their partner. Do not divide them. They are a family.

* Compliment their strengths as a couple. Offer words of encouragement rather than unsolicited advice, and let them know that you believe in their choices.

* Consider multiple ways of showing support, and ask your adult child and their partner how they'd like to receive support. Remember that not everyone feels love through gifts or words of affirmation.

* You are all responsible for communicating with one another and for your dynamic. Take ownership for your part. Instead of expecting them to change, be the one to change first.

* As your adult child and partner grow into their own family, do not try to separate them or put pressure on your child to

choose you over their partner. This doesn't work and will only hurt your relationship. If you're concerned about the health of their relationship, consider showing your child what it means to connect in a healthy way by going for walks and having dinners together. Be a listening ear, but not a persuading problem solver. Encourage them to seek therapy, either individually or as a couple. Don't play the role of therapist or give advice on whether they should stay or go; this will backfire and could result in blame on you.

* Although it might be difficult, accept that there will be differences in the way your adult child and partner spend time with you versus the way they spend time with the partner's family. Avoid comparisons and focus on nurturing your own bond with both your adult child and their partner.

* When becoming a grandparent, recognize that you had your turn as a parent, and now it's your child and their partner's turn. Allow them to experience their firsts without you giving unsolicited opinions or advice. This is not your chance to fix mistakes or make up for lost time through your grandchildren. New parents need encouragement and validation, statements like "You're doing great" and "I trust you've got this."

* When your adult child and their partner are new parents, they need you to support *them* during this big transition in their life, not just the baby. Ask them how they're doing before asking if their baby is sleeping through the night.

* When your grandchildren get older, follow their parents' guidelines. Don't engage in "splitting"-type comments (e.g., "Mommy doesn't allow this, but it's okay with Grandma" or "Grandma does it best").

* Continue to nurture your own identity, relationships, and interests outside of family life. In our society, women are praised for staying at home and focusing on children. Now is the time to find joy, creativity, and play for you, your relationships, and your hobbies. When you become a grandparent, there can be a pull to resume a focus on babies. Balance nurturing your family bond with remaining connected to your community.

FOR YOUR HUSBAND: FIVE TIPS FOR ENGAGING IN THE VAULT METHOD

So your partner passed you this book. Maybe you're on the precipice of an important event, like getting married or welcoming a baby. Or maybe you've hit some bumps in the road with your wife and your mother, and something needs to change. Perhaps you're on board with your wife and understand her feelings. Or perhaps you're struggling to see what the problem is. Either way, I've built the VAULT method to help both of you get to a place where you feel good about your relationship with each other and good about the relationship you're building with your mother as a couple. VAULT stands for Values, Aspirations, Understanding Your Triangle, Limits and Boundaries, and Taking Action. This system is not about creating divides or cutting people out. It's about giving you and your wife the tools to communicate and come to a place with your mother that feels good for both of you.

The role of partnership is to practice prioritizing each other, knowing each other deeply, and putting the health of your relationship first. I can't emphasize enough that if one partner is struggling with something, then the entire relationship is struggling. If your partner has an issue with something, it also becomes your issue to work through. That doesn't necessarily mean you agree with her about the issue, but it means you will honor her feelings, grow curious and compassionate about her struggle, and work together to be a connected and collaborative team.

Your loyalty to your wife is essential for your relationship with your mother to improve. The relationship between your wife and mother will not improve when you don't side with your wife. I know this can be tricky, but it's what the VAULT method is here to help you do. And over the next few pages, I'll go over five tips to help you make the process as smooth and effective as possible.

1. CREATE AN ADULT RELATIONSHIP WITH YOUR MOTHER

I work with many men who, as they deal with the stresses of work and daily life, default to letting their partner take over "kin keeping," or nurturing family ties. The wife ends up handling communication, event planning, and gift buying, not just with her family of origin but with her husband's as well. Eventually, it can get to the point where your mother is texting your wife instead of you about everything—not just the best time to visit the grandkids but whether you're watching your cholesterol and whether you've read the book she gave you for your birthday.

As an adult, you're responsible for working on respectful adult relationships with everyone in your life, including your mother. This responsibility doesn't pass to your wife when you get married. It's imperative that you take ownership over the relationship with your mom, including replying to her texts in a timely manner and being involved with coordinating events, as you would with any adult. This also means making decisions about what you share with her, how frequently you contact her, and how often you see her, in ways you and your partner agree on when identifying your values and aspirations as part of the VAULT method.

2. DON'T PUT YOUR PARTNER IN THE ROLE OF MOTHER

Part of creating an adult relationship with your mother is understanding that as an adult, you are responsible for taking initiative. If you say you'll text your mother, you text her without having to be reminded. If you agree to set a boundary with your mother that reflects your and your partner's values as a couple, you set it. You treat your partner as an equal with you, not as a mother who has to nag her son to do his chores.

Many men tell me, "I try to do it, but I forget." If this is a common scenario, it tells me you need to find a new system to complete the task. Ask yourself: How do you remember to do things at your job or in other areas of life that are important to you? If you need to set reminders in your calendar or write a to-do list, do so. One strategy I like from James Clear's *Atomic Habits* is to "pair an action you *want* to do with an action you *need* to do."[1] For example: "Before I can buy the thing I want online, I need to purchase my mom's birthday gift" or "Before I can scroll on social media, I need to text my mom back."

3. REMEMBER THAT DESIRE IS CONNECTED TO EVERY ASPECT OF YOUR RELATIONSHIP

I see many heterosexual couples show up to therapy complaining about not having sex. While there can be a mismatch in levels of desire between two partners, it's important to remember that sex does not exist in a vacuum separate from the rest of a relationship. Every moment of connection or disconnection between two people can affect their respective levels of desire and willingness to say yes or no to sexual intimacy.

If your wife is carrying the weight of the mental load of going to work, caring for the kids, and managing all the communication with your parents, it will probably affect her feelings of desire negatively. If she feels disconnected from you because your mom criticized her and you didn't say anything, it will probably affect her feelings of desire negatively. Conversely, if you set a boundary with your mother, or if you ease the burden of her mental load by saying, "I've got the gifts covered for my family this year," it might have the opposite effect and lead your wife to feel more connected to you.

4. VALIDATE YOUR WIFE'S EXPERIENCE, ABOVE ALL ELSE

I get it. You feel pulled between two women in your life. You ask yourself, "Should I upset my wife and please my mother? Or upset my mother and please my wife?" Since you're used to your long-standing patterns with your mother, you may have come to see her behavior as the status quo. The status quo seems impossible to change, so you turn to your partner and ask her to change instead. (For example, you might say something like "That's just my mom," excusing your mom's behavior and its impact on your wife and family.) In the process of this (often unconscious) decision, you end up denying or minimizing your wife's experience, which leaves her feeling alone and disconnected.

Research shows couples feel more satisfied if husbands are on the same page as their wives about the husband's mother's behavior.[2] You don't have to agree with everything she says or villainize your mother, but validating your wife's experience will help you both feel more connected and like a team. I know at times your wife might come to you saying something hurtful about your mother. While you don't need to condone attacks on your mother's personality, you can try to reframe the moment to see the emotion that your wife is feeling. Underneath her potentially hurtful words are pain and sadness that her mother-in-law isn't who she hoped she would be, and that her relationship with you is hurting because of it.

5. RECOGNIZING THE PROBLEM IS THE FIRST STEP TO SOLVING IT

We engage in avoidance and denial when we don't want to deal with hard information or difficult experiences. The guilt trip your mother gave you last week, the hurtful comment she made about your parenting choices, the repeated criticisms of your wife—you might just put them all in a box and try not to think about them. As one male client put it, "I have a storage unit of boxes that I just haven't looked at in years." While these are useful ways of protecting your feelings in the short term, in the long run, you end up building layers of resentment, confusion, and hurt—for yourself, for your partner, *and* for your mother. This is why doing nothing is not avoiding the problem—it's actually making the problem worse. The longer you deny that a problem exists, the harder it becomes to repair these relationships.

My client Stephanie spent twelve years trying to get her husband, Philip, to see just how hurtful his mother's behavior was. Philip kept repeating, "It's just who she is" and "You need a thicker skin." Like Philip, you might have become desensitized to your mom's actions. Having lived with them your whole life, you might see them as "normal." But just because you're used to a problem doesn't mean it's not a problem. Ignoring it may have worked well enough for you when you were single, but now that your wife is in the picture, it doesn't work anymore. That doesn't mean you should aim to change your mother; rather, the goal is to be on the same team as your wife, acting as a united couple. This might involve asserting your needs with your mother, asking your mother to stop making critical comments, or setting boundaries. It will not involve pretending everything is fine.

By accepting that there is actually a problem in your relationships with your wife and your mother, you are taking the first step in doing something different. As Philip told me, he wished he had addressed his own struggles with boundaries a decade before arriving at my office. I won't forget his words, so I want to share them with you: "Perhaps my relationship with my mother would be different today if I had done this work earlier. This is something that I will have to grieve about my own choices."

NOTES

Introduction

1. Esposito, Leigh (@msleighesposito), "The Biggest Threat to Italian Marriages," *Instagram*, posted September 20, 2023, accessed September 16, 2024, https://www.instagram.com/reel/CxbMxMDR4gW/. Janelle Marie (@heyjanellemarie), "Daughter-in-Law Math," *Instagram*, posted October 28, 2023, accessed September 16, 2024, https://www.instagram.com/reel/Cy9CEC4g5SE/.

Chapter 1: A Special Kind of Relationship

1. Bowen, Murray, *Family Therapy in Clinical Practice* (Jason Aronson, 1978).

Chapter 2: The Family You Join

1. White, Martha A., Janice H. Elder, Eija Paavilainen, Katja Joronen, Halla L. Helgadóttir, and Annette Seidl, "Family Dynamics in the United States, Finland, and Iceland," *Scandinavian Journal of Caring Sciences* 24, no. 1 (March 2010): 84–93, DOI: 10.1111/j.1471-6712.2009.00689.x.

2. Rittenour, Christine, "Daughter-in-Law Standards for Mother-in-Law Communication: Associations with Daughter-in-Law Perceptions of Relational Satisfaction and Shared Family Identity," *Journal of Family Communication* 12, no. 2 (2012): 93–110, https://doi.org/10.1080/15267431.2010.537240.

3. Strauss, Maximilian, and Marco Battaglia, "Childhood Separation Anxiety: Human and Preclinical Studies," in *Separation Anxiety in Adulthood*, November 24, 2023, 5–28, https://doi.org/10.1007/978-3-031-37446-3_2.

4. Zahrakar, Kianoush, Farshad Lavafpour, and Farshad Mohsenzadeh, "Exploring Factors Affecting Conflict Between Daughter-in-Law and Mother-in-Law: A Qualitative Study," *International Journal of Health Sciences* 6, no. S7 (2022): 48338–65, https://doi.org/10.53730/ijhs.v6nS7.13521.

5. Miklas, Margie, "Mammoni and Mammismo: An Italian Lifestyle," *Margie in Italy*, May 2017, accessed August 25, 2024, https://margieinitaly.com/2017/05/mammoni-and-mammismo-an-italian-lifestyle/.

6. Fingerman, Karen L., Megan Gilligan, Laura VanderDrift, and Lindsay Pitzer, "In-Law Relationships Before and After Marriage," *Research in Human Development* 9, no. 2 (2012): 106–25, https://doi.org/10.1080/15427609.2012.680843.

7. Everri, Marina, Tiziana Mancini, and Laura Fruggeri, "The Role of Rigidity in Adaptive and Maladaptive Families Assessed by FACES IV: The Points of View of Adolescents," *Journal of Child and Family Studies* 25, no. 10 (2016): 2987–97, https://doi.org/10.1007/s10826-016-0460-3.

8. Serewicz, Mary Clare Morr, and Robert A. Hosmer, "In-Laws or Outlaws: The Dark and the Bright in In-Law Relationships," in *The Dark Side of Close Relationships II*, ed. William R. Cupach and Brian H. Spitzberg (Routledge, 2011), 217–42.

9. Serewicz and Hosmer, "In-Laws or Outlaws."

10. Karpman, Stephen B, M.D., *A Game Free Life: The Definitive Book on the Drama Triangle and Compassion Triangle by the Originator and Author: The New Transactional Analysis of Intimacy, Openness, and Happiness* (Drama Triangle Productions, 2019).

11. Gruhn, Meredith A., and Bruce E. Compas, "Effects of Maltreatment on Coping and Emotion Regulation in Childhood and Adolescence: A Meta-Analytic Review," *Child Abuse & Neglect* 123 (2022): 105377, https://doi.org/10.1016/j.chiabu.2021.105377.

12. Gabay, Rahav, Boaz Hameiri, Tammy Rubel-Lifschitz, and Arie Nadler, "The Tendency for Interpersonal Victimhood: The Personality Construct and Its Consequences," *Personality and Individual Differences* 165 (2020): 110134, https://doi.org/10.1016/j.paid.2020.110134.

13. Gibson, Lindsay C., *Adult Children of Emotionally Immature Parents: How to Heal from Distant, Rejecting, or Self-Involved Parents* (New Harbinger Publications, 2015).

Chapter 3: Addressing Our Own Baggage

1. Fingerman, Karen L., Megan Gilligan, Laura VanderDrift, and Lindsay Pitzer, "In-Law Relationships Before and After Marriage," *Research in Human Development* 9, no. 2 (2012): 106–25.

2. McNulty, James K., "Should Spouses Be Demanding Less from Marriage? A Contextual Perspective on the Implications of Interpersonal Standards," *Personality and Social Psychology Bulletin* 42, no. 4 (2016): 444–57, https://doi.org/10.1177/0146167216634050.

3. Rittenour, Christine, "Daughter-in-Law Standards for Mother-in-Law Communication: Associations with Daughter-in-Law Perceptions of Relational Satisfaction and Shared Family Identity," *Journal of Family Communication* 12, no. 2 (2012): 93–110, https://doi.org/10.1080/15267431.2010.537240.

4. Rittenour, Christine E., and Jody Koenig Kellas, "Making Sense of Hurtful Mother-in-Law Messages: Applying Attribution Theory to the In-Law Triad," *Communication Quarterly* 63, no. 1 (2015): 62–80, https://doi.org/10.1080/01463373.2014.965837.

Chapter 4: From "You Versus Me" to "We"

1. Johnson, Susan M. *The Practice of Emotionally Focused Couple Therapy: Creating Connection,* 3rd ed. (Routledge, 2019).

2. Siegel, Daniel J, *Mindsight: The New Science of Personal Transformation* (Bantam Books, 2010), 26, 31, 35.

3. Elliott, Robert, Jeanne C. Watson, Rhonda N. Goldman, and Leslie S. Greenberg, *Learning Emotion-Focused Therapy: The Process-Experiential Approach to Change* (American Psychological Association, 2009), 29.

4. Goldman, Rhonda N., and Ian C. Wise, "Secondary Reactive Emotions in Emotion-Focused Therapy," in *Encyclopedia of Couple and Family Therapy,* ed. James L. Lebow, Anthony L. Chambers, and Douglas C. Breunlin (Springer, 2019), https://doi.org/10.1007/978-3-319-49425-8_203.

5. Gottman, John, and Julie Schwartz Gottman, *Fight Right: How Successful Couples Turn Conflict into Connection* (Harmony Books, 2024), 13.

6. Tronick, Edward, *The Still Face Experiment,* video produced by the Child Development Media, 2007.

7. Gottman and Gottman, *Fight Right*, 164.

Chapter 5: Values

1. Harris, Russ, *The Happiness Trap: How to Stop Struggling and Start Living* (Shambhala, 2008), 5.

2. Davis, KC, *How to Keep House While Drowning: A Gentle Approach to Cleaning and Organizing* (S&S/Simon Element, 2022), 11.

3. Carr, Barb, "Live Your Core Values: 10-Minute Exercise to Increase Your Success," *TapRooT® Root Cause Analysis*, April 11, 2013, https://taproot.com/live-your-core-values-exercise-to-increase-your-success/.

4. Harris, *Happiness Trap*, 35.

5. Gottlieb, Lori, *Maybe You Should Talk to Someone: A Therapist, Her Therapist, and Our Lives Revealed* (Houghton Mifflin Harcourt, 2019), 153.

Chapter 6: Aspirations

1. Dana, Deb, *Polyvagal Theory in Therapy: Engaging the Rhythm of Regulation* (W. W. Norton, 2018), 15.

2. Bowen, Murray, *Family Therapy in Clinical Practice* (Jason Aronson, 1978).

3. Brach, Tara, *Radical Compassion: Learning to Love Yourself and Your World with the Practice of RAIN* (Viking, 2019), 4.

4. Robbins, Mel, *The Let Them Theory: A Life-Changing Tool That Millions of People Can't Stop Talking About* (Hay House, 2024), 38.

5. Kessler, David, *Finding Meaning: The Sixth Stage of Grief* (Scribner, 2019).

6. Wile, Daniel B., "Dan's Quotes," *Dan's Blog*, accessed September 30, 2024, https://danwile.com/my-blog/my-quotes/.

7. Gottman, John M., and Robert W. Levenson, "What Predicts Change in Marital Interaction Over Time? A Study of Alternative Models," *Family Process* 38, no. 2 (July 28, 2004): 143–58, https://doi.org/10.1111/j.1545-5300.1999.00143.x.

8. Gottman, John M., "A Theory of Marital Dissolution and Stability," *Journal of Family Psychology* 7, no. 1 (1993): 57–75, https://doi.org/10.1037/0893-3200.7.1.57.

9. Gottman, John, and Julie Schwartz Gottman, *Fight Right: How Successful Couples Turn Conflict into Connection* (Harmony Books, 2024), 318.

Chapter 7: Understanding Your Triangle

1. Bowen, Murray, *Family Therapy in Clinical Practice* (Jason Aronson, 1978).

2. Neff, Kristin D., "Self-Compassion: An Alternative Conceptualization of a Healthy Attitude Toward Oneself," *Self and Identity* 2, no. 2 (2003): 85–101, https://doi.org/10.1080/15298860309032.

3. Rittenour, Christine, and Jordan Soliz, "Communicative and Relational Dimensions of Shared Family Identity and Relational Intentions in Mother-in-Law/Daughter-in-Law Relationships: Developing a Conceptual Model for Mother-in-Law/Daughter-in-Law Research," *Western Journal of Communication* 73, no. 1 (January–March 2009): 67–90, published online February 9, 2009, https://doi.org/10.1080/10570310802636334; Rittenour, Christine E., and Jody Koenig Kellas, "Making Sense of Hurtful Mother-in-Law Messages: Applying Attribution Theory to the In-Law Triad," *Communication Quarterly* 63, no. 1 (2015): 62–80, https://doi.org/10.1080/01463373.2014.965837.

Chapter 8: Limits and Boundaries

1. Tawwab, Nedra Glover, *Set Boundaries, Find Peace: A Guide to Reclaiming Yourself* (TarcherPerigee, 2021), 12.

2. Miller, William R., and Stephen Rollnick, *Motivational Interviewing: Helping People Change*, 3rd ed. (Guilford Press, 2013), 74.

3. Dalgleish, Tracy (Host), "Decoding Personalization with the Shrink Chicks," *Dear Dr. Tracy* podcast, November 9, 2023, accessed January 1, 2025, https://podcasts.apple.com/ca/podcast/decoding-personalization-with-the-shrink-chicks/id1452433255?i=1000634247801.

Chapter 9: Taking Action

1. HIGH5 Content & Review Team, HIGH5 Test, *Strengths* blog, "Personal Strengths & Weaknesses: Guide & List with 90 Strengths," February 27, 2024, accessed November 23, 2024, https://high5test.com/personal-strengths-list/.

2. Kennedy, Becky, *Good Inside: A Guide to Becoming the Parent You Want to Be* (Harper Wave, 2022), 4.

3. Ball, Hannah, Keith Weber, Alan K. Goodboy, Christine E. Kunkle, Christa L. Lilly, and Scott A. Myers, "A Mixed Methodological Examination of Older Adults' Psychological Reactance Toward Caregiving Messages from Their Adult Children," *Communication Monographs* 90, no. 2 (2022): 137–58, doi:10.1080/03637751.2022.2128197.

Chapter 10: Putting It into Practice

1. Rittenour, Christine, and Jordan Soliz, "Communicative and Relational Dimensions of Shared Family Identity and Relational Intentions in Mother-in-Law/Daughter-in-Law Relationships: Developing a Conceptual Model for Mother-in-Law/Daughter-in-Law Research," *Western Journal of Communication* 73, no. 1 (January–March 2009): 67–90, published online February 9, 2009, https://doi.org/10.1080/10570310802636334.

Appendix A

1. Rittenour, Christine, and Jordan Soliz, "Communicative and Relational Dimensions of Shared Family Identity and Relational Intentions in Mother-in-Law/Daughter-in-Law Relationships: Developing a Conceptual Model for Mother-in-Law/Daughter-in-Law Research," *Western Journal of Communication* 73, no. 1 (January–March 2009): 67–90, published online February 9, 2009, https://doi.org/10.1080/10570310802636334.

Appendix B

1. Clear, James, *Atomic Habits: An Easy & Proven Way to Build Good Habits & Break Bad Ones* (Avery, 2018), 212.

2. Rittenour, Christine E., and Jody Koenig Kellas, "Making Sense of Hurtful Mother-in-Law Messages: Applying Attribution Theory to the In-Law Triad," *Communication Quarterly* 63, no. 1 (2015): 62–80, https://doi.org/10.1080/01463373.2014.965837.

INDEX